WISDOM FROM THE JAZZMAN

Smooth Words To Help You Navigate Through Life

JAY LANG

NEW YORK

VIRGINIA

Wisdom From The Jazzman
Jay Lang

ISBN 9781938467240

Published by

 köehlerbooks™

an imprint of Morgan James Publishing

5 Penn Plaza, 23rd floor
c/o Morgan James Publishing
New York, NY 10001
212-574-7939
www.koehlerbooks.com

Publisher
John Köehler

Executive Editor
Joe Coccaro

Contents

"The world is full of abundance and opportunity, but far too many people come to the fountain of life with a sieve instead of a tank car... a teaspoon instead of a steam shovel. They expect little and as a result they get little."

— Ben Sweetland, author and psychologist

Introduction

Life is a fantastic journey with many twists and turns. Once you realize there are no straight lines, you'll be a lot better prepared for what's ahead. As you travel life's road and navigate its sharp curves, potholes, and bumps, share that experience to help others following behind you. That is a major key that will open up many doors to opportunity and success in life.

Listeners repeatedly told me how they want to hear the truth, no matter how much it hurts or how jarring. They want companions, friends, children, co-workers, family, and spouses to be honest with them. When I say "need to hear it," I mean we need to really hear the truth about who we are, what we're becoming, what we do, how the world sees us, how we carry ourselves, how our actions affect others and, most of all, how to reach our spiritual and earthly potential. The reason so many of us never achieve our destinies is because we get sidetracked or too caught up in the world. We can become selfish, blinded by ego or pain, making it difficult to see ourselves realistically and truthfully. Simply put, "Life gets in the way."

I have been in that trap and have fortunately escaped. I'm just like you—a regular hardworking person with faults and dreams. I have been blessed with the ability to sometimes see things before they happen and observe life for what it really is. I have benefited from the wisdom of my elders, my family, and the people who helped me in my career and provided necessary tools. Get focused, and stay focused. It's not hard. You just have to put your mind to it and do it. Remain open to possibilities that present themselves and always be willing to listen, absorb, and learn. Others often see us better than we see ourselves.

Part of my destiny and focus is to share my observations on life and suggest how to improve your life in every respect. This motivational book will inspire you to change and to guide that course correction if you put these lessons into practice each day. Consider it a bodybuilding of the mind. Read it over and over again, and keep it close to you in times of need or when no one else can help you. Always remember that you are wonderful, fantastic, and your true life purpose awaits.

As you begin this journey with me, prepare to accept the possibilities and wake up to the enormously new, wonderful, successful, beautiful person God has created within you. Throughout my life I have written poems, songs, magazine articles, and news to help find that better person in myself and others. I learned much from the wisdom of my father, Southern radio legend Jimmy "The Gator" Lang, and from my family, pastors, and teachers, all of whom were inspired by a desire to help others. Am I a doctor? No. A psychologist? No. A minister? No, although many have said that was my calling. I am an individual just like you, blessed with certain talents and skills. I consider myself a caring man with a helping heart. The lessons learned in your life's journey through the words contained in these pages are ultimately from someone bigger than you and me. I am just the vessel used to reveal them to you. For that, I am thankful.

My *Wisdom From The Jazzman* journey began as a nightly feature on my radio show in Norfolk, Virginia, at WJCD Smooth Jazz 105.3. The show at that time was "Lights Out Hampton Roads." I needed a feature that would capture the attention of listeners in search of wisdom, something that would draw them back each night. My career and my destiny intersected when I filled an afternoon drive position in Washington, D.C., at WJZW Smooth Jazz 105.9. The transition from Norfolk to a top ten major market was a wonderful journey filled with many lessons, good people, and blessings. Being the first African American Smooth Jazz air personality in Afternoon Drive on that station proved profitable in many ways, but more so than that, it began the real journey toward capturing life experiences—not only my life, but the lives of others.

After a few years achieving ratings success in the afternoons, I transitioned to nights, which management felt was the right fit for my more seasoned and soothing voice. I also had more freedom to connect with my listeners. When I worked nights, I could shop during the day while everyone else was working; I could work out in the health club and not have to worry about crowds. I had more time to develop my other business interests. There was a lot of upside to this idea. I wasn't married, and it would give me time to get involved actively with my First Baptist Church of Glenarden family and ministries. So I made the move. This was the birth of "Lights Out Washington."

This transition gave me the opportunity to resurrect two radio features I loved dearly: "Romantic Recipes" and "Words of Wisdom." They became daily writings that I shared each night with my Washington, Maryland, and northern Virginia audience. The more I wrote them and spoke to my audience, the more response I received. The e-mails of gratitude became more frequent. The calls of thanks grew. People began to stop me on the street just to let me know how much they loved those two segments.

Listeners from around the world, using the Internet, began to tune in to hear what I would share. That feedback inspired me to write more. But it was on the days when I had nothing to talk about, the days when what was revealed to my listeners didn't really come from me, that I knew this was bigger than me. It was God using me to help them. The messages were therapeutic. Too often we repeat mistakes by failing to listen to those around us. If we do listen, we fail to hear. We allow life to live us instead of us living it. Sometimes you are just too close to the issues surrounding you. It's like holding a book two inches from your eyes. All of the answers are there, but you can't see them because you're too close to the text. You have to pull away from the pages to be able to make out the lettering, to read the whole chapter, and absorb its content. Hopefully these writings will pull you away from what you're currently experiencing so you too can see where you are and where you should be.

We have one shot at life, no second show, no encore, no reruns. So, live it to the fullest, and let the journey toward your destiny begin: a destiny that's filled with increasing common sense and knowledge of the most important thing of all—life.

Life

"Life is full of beauty. Notice it.

Notice the bumblebee, the small child,

and the smiling faces. Smell the rain, and feel the wind.

Live your life to the fullest potential,

and fight for your dreams."

— Ashley Smith

My life has been filled with the colors of special moments, memories, laughter, and unspeakable joys, some of which I once failed to recognize but appreciate fully now. I grew up in an entertainment household where famous celebrities like James Brown were referred to as Uncle James. He was a very close friend to my father during his heyday in radio in the 1960s and 1970s and through his final years. Augusta, Georgia, was only "a ways up the road" as they often say down South. James Brown and The Famous Flames, along with other black groups, performed at the Savannah Sports Arena on weekends. African Americans were only allowed to use the facility after the wrestling matches, which was roughly around eleven at night. Friendly as it was in my eyes, it was still the segregated South. Back then, five dollars would get you admission and a "set up," two cups and some ice for your drinks. Sodas were a dime, but most patrons brought their own bottles, known to this day as BYOB. When the lights went down and Mr. Dynamite hit the stage, that was all she wrote. Women screaming, brothers dancing, and people partying like there was not a problem in the world.

During afternoons prior to the shows at the arena, bands would often rehearse in our garage. We lived in an upper-middle-class neighborhood in the only house on the block with a garage. My dad offered it as a safe haven for black musicians who were not allowed to warm up in the arena before a show because of segregation issues. I had no idea at the time that I was in the midst of musical superstars, musicians who played with legends including B.B. King, Sam Cooke, Otis Redding, Johnny Ace, Jackie Wilson, and so many more. I was living in an entertainment wonderland and didn't even know it. All I knew was I could dance until I got sleepy from the music coming from only a few feet away through thin walls of sheetrock and wood. My love for music was born while sitting on the laps of friends while Dad promoted those concerts after working all week at radio station WSOK.

I mention that particular period in my life because it left a mark on me. Life will leave impressions, memories good and bad, and scars—and that is to be expected. How you live life is what's most important. Enjoy its many colors; live it to the fullest.

Encourage Yourself

Wouldn't it be great to have someone providing you with a constant supply of encouragement? Well, when you get in the habit of encouraging yourself, that's exactly what you can have. All day long, you think and say things to yourself. You have the power to choose precisely what those thoughts and those words will be.

Choose to make them positive, uplifting, and encouraging. Make good use of the thousands of opportunities you have each day to provide yourself with support and direction. When you catch yourself mentally beating up on yourself, decide then and there to stop. How's that helping the situation? It's not. Maybe you don't get encouragement at home or at work. So what? Give yourself a few words of real, sincere encouragement.

Instead of talking about someone who has fallen short, get in the habit of offering encouragement to those you come in contact with whenever you get the chance. What goes around comes around. That'll make them more likely to send encouragement your way. Don't depend on the world to encourage you. Pat yourself on the back when you need it.

Enjoy Life

Make up your mind right now to enjoy life. Stop deceiving yourself into believing and thinking that you have to get away from your daily routine in order to truly relax and enjoy life. Don't wait for your next vacation or next paycheck. Enjoy today and every day as a precious gift from God.

Enjoy getting up and eating breakfast. Enjoy going to work. Enjoy mowing the lawn. Enjoy the sunsets and moonlight. Enjoy going to the grocery store. Enjoy washing the dishes. Enjoy your children and family. You do these things anyway, so why not choose to enjoy them? When you do, you will go through life with a smile on your face, a spring in your step, and you'll enjoy the abundant, overflowing life of victory intended for you. And don't ever set yourself up for disappointment by expecting someone else to be your source of joy. It's totally up to you.

Realize that although it's not necessarily planned, people can sometimes let you down and bring you down if you let them. Decide right now not to let that happen to you anymore. In essence, you don't have to necessarily change what you do, just change your attitude toward what you do. Let this be your moment of liberation. Tomorrow is but a promise hoped for. So enjoy today. Enjoy the world around you, each and every day from this day forward.

Watch What You Say

Words set the direction for your life. Which direction are you going? Are you declaring good things, speaking words of faith over your future? Or are you going around saying negative things. Your words have great power.

Use the words you speak to declare good things. Declare victory over the difficulties and obstacles in your life. Declare good health. Declare joy. Declare prosperity. Get up every day and boldly declare, "This is going to be a great day. I may have been defeated in the past, but this is a new day. God is on my side. Things are changing in my favor. Today is going to be the best day of my life." Even if it doesn't turn out the way you expected it to, it was still a good day because you gave it your all and learned something from it that you can use to move forward another day. Think before you speak. Listen well and completely before you respond in conversation. Your words have great power. Power to hurt others. Power to lift up. Power to bring you down. Power to move you to greatness. Besides all that, you can apologize, but once you say it, once the words leave your lips, you can't take them back. Watch what you say.

Give And You'll Receive

One of the main hindrances to prosperity is selfishness. If you live life selfishly, focusing only on your wants and needs, you'll never be able to experience the best life has waiting for you. As the biblical verse says, "Whatsoever a man sows, that he will also reap." In other words, in order to prosper, you've got to learn how to be a giver.

For a flower to grow, you have to plant a seed, cultivate and water it. Then it needs sun and fertilizer to grow. You have to feed that flower to reveal its full beauty. Do nothing for it, and it'll wither and die. The same applies to life. You must give of your time, energy, and resources to others in need in order to receive. Just like a farmer, you have to plant good seeds in order to receive a good harvest. Help others when you can and expect the best. To get blessings, you have to be a blessing.

Begin to plant those good seeds in your life by simply giving to others. If nothing else, be a little less self-centered by giving of your time and encouragement, and soon you'll see good things begin to flow in your life like running waters. You've tried everything else on the road to prosperity and happiness; why not try giving and you'll receive more than you'll ever believe.

Stand Strong

If you're having negative or discouraging feelings, shake them off as soon as they start. Even if you don't feel like it, choose to rule over that negative feeling anyway. Thinking negative and feeling discouraged cannot, does not, and never will improve a situation. If you can't do it alone then call a positive, motivating friend. Those of us in the positive circle of thinkers will be more than happy to keep you encouraged and focused on the bright side of life. Tell yourself: I'm going to be steady, immovable, and full of joy, regardless of my circumstances. Regardless of what someone says or does. Regardless of what happens today or tomorrow. The more you say this to yourself, the easier it will become. If you're in the middle of a crisis, stop being so quick to give up and give in. Stay positive. Explore your options. None of us has control over the unexpected things that come our way, so you have to stand strong. Only you can change you. Expect the unexpected. Today and every day, decide to be a more stable person, refuse to give negativity and discouragement a place in your life. Start enjoying your life—all of it!

Decide To Be Happy

Unhappy? Not where you feel you should or want to be? If certain things in your life were just a little bit "better," would you be happy? A better job, a better house, better health, more money, a better relationship?

The truth is it only takes one thing for you to be happy. It takes a made up mind. That's right! You have to decide that you are going to be happy regardless of your situation. Sure, you may have some obstacles to overcome, but don't ever let that steal your joy. Like my grandmother always said: "Son, trouble don't last always." So begin each day thinking of all the things you have to be thankful for.

Decide each morning to declare to yourself, "I'm going to enjoy this day and be happy regardless of what comes my way." If you don't get happy where you are, you'll never get to where you want to be. It all begins with a grateful attitude toward life. Don't say you don't have anything to be thankful for. If you can hear me now, you have something to be thankful for. Learn to be content with life regardless of your circumstances. When you do, you'll start living an abundant, joy-filled life, and blessings will come your way. Try it this week and see the difference a new "attitude of gratitude" will make.

What's Done Is Done

The time and energy you spend complaining about things you cannot change will bring you nothing but a lot of frustration, stress, and negativity. What's happened has happened. Instead of looking back, fretting, and arguing about why or how or who is at fault, look forward and consider all the positive possibilities that are available to you.

If you've been done wrong, don't seek revenge. Seek success, seek achievement, seek fulfillment, seek to take what has happened and turn it into a positive force in your life. Spend your time and energy not in looking back, but in looking ahead, because that's where you can make a difference. You can't change the past, but you can design your future.

Learn from what has happened; allow it to inspire and motivate you in a positive way, and then choose to move forward. See the value in the way things are at this moment, and see how you can make full use of that value. Let go of your attachment to what has already happened. It's unchangeable history. You'll never be able to change the past, so move on and make room in your life to create the very best that can be.

Think First

We all have the tendency to act on impulse. It has its benefits, but it also has very negative results. Think of a situation where you've said something that's caused you grief or embarrassment afterward. Words are powerful. Use yours wisely. Sometimes it's best to keep quiet. Think before you speak your mind.

When you finally realize you can't say whatever you want in every situation, you'll end up a better person. On your job, you can't speak your mind in every situation unless you're prepared to deal with the consequences. It can get you fired. It's what we say that so often gets us in trouble. Saying what you feel at the wrong time can cause more problems. Think before you fly off the handle just because someone had an opinion contrary to yours; before you bite back when you think someone's wrong; before you say something you think instead of finding out the facts; before you speak ill or lies about someone.

Sometimes you have to take two steps back before you can move forward. Delay will enable you to see how to get yourself back on a positive path. So don't move so fast, and don't speak so quickly. Once you've said it, you can't take it back. So slow down.

Lighten Up

Are you the kind of person who never gets the joke? Always so serious about things? Life is a wonderful journey with many things to laugh and smile about. No matter how successful you are, if you're serious all the time you're living a rather boring life. Live a little. Try some new things. Take some time to play and laugh. Ever wonder why you're always being told about but never invited to parties or social outings? It's because you're too stiff, boring, and dull. You're not really living life, life is living you. You're getting older, so get out, be more active, go places, do new things. Enjoy life.

If you relax your attitude, you'll find yourself getting more done, meeting nice people, and finding wonderful new opportunities. Face it: It's no fun dealing with people who have no personality, no sense of humor, and who are serious about business all the time. You have to try extra hard to get to know them, make friends, or do business. You can be successful and happy at the same time, so don't take life so seriously. God gave us the ability to laugh for a reason. It's food for the soul. Laugh a little, and enjoy this wonderful world around you. You have so many things to be happy about. Recognize them.

Exhale

We take too many things seriously to the point of extreme stress. Too many worries about job and family. Too many worries about bills we really shouldn't have made in the first place. You created that problem, and now you're stressing about it. You just had to have it, didn't you? Or so you think. Now something unexpected has drained your finances. Stop fretting, and deal with it. Confront the problem, and you'll shed the stress too. Exhale.

First step, work out an action plan to get that problem taken care of and stick to it. Stop avoiding the bill collector's phone calls and ignoring the mail. They'll just keep coming. Running away is no way to live. Face the issue, and work out a plan to get it taken care of in a way that's comfortable, but only promise to pay what you can afford. If you stick to it, you'll get it behind you. Just make sure you don't get back into that mess again. If you address problems and solve them, instead of running and hiding you'll eliminate the stress and enable yourself to think clearly and enjoy life.

Make a solid decision once and for all to change your life's direction and live within your physical, financial, and emotional means. If you have to drop people out of your life, change careers, relocate, or take a stand, just do it. Life's too short to stress out about the temporary things.

Wake Up

Sometimes life throws you a curve. Something happens that hits you from nowhere. It probably happened when everything was just beginning to go your way. When it does, it can devastate your world and mess up your mind, even throw you into depression. You lose your momentum and balance. When the unexpected traumas of life hit, don't let them cloud your focus. Are you the person everyone comes to when they need to be lifted mentally and emotionally, yet when you need the same thing, you can't get yourself up? An accident, drastic employment change, emotional shock, family crisis, or a financial setback will pull you out of character and cause you to panic if you let it. When a crisis comes, that's when you need to lean on your faith and put into practice the many encouraging words you've passed along to others in their time of need.

Snap out of it! Keep moving forward; stop moping; stop procrastinating. Put on the emotional and spiritual armor you've been blessed with and fight back. As I've said before, if you're striving to live a righteous life, bad times come to make you stronger. If you get up, stay positive and keep on pushing. You'll get through it and come out on the other side stronger, wiser, and better than before. So don't let it get you down, hold you back, and cause you to forget who you are and what you're capable of. This too shall pass.

Look At The Bright Side

Life throws you curves from time to time. When the unexpected comes, you have a choice as to how you'll react. You can fall apart, adding emotional stress to the situation, or you can realize that things can and will happen in your life as long as you live and stay positive. In every situation, there is a bright side.

If you've lost your job, instead of being depressed, be thankful that you saved something to get you through this to the next one. If you don't have anything saved, be thankful you have your health and the strength to be able to find a new job, and get to finding one now instead of sulking about it. Maybe you've been transferred unexpectedly. Instead of being upset, be happy about the opportunity to start life over in a new place with new friends, leaving your present unpleasant situations behind. Shed the bad; seek out the good.

If you're going through an illness, be thankful that you have the faith and strength to get through it. Lost the one you love to someone else? Be happy it happened, because obviously it wasn't meant to be. Now you can find someone who really loves you, instead of someone pretending to love you. You wouldn't have been happy in that situation anyway. I could go on with examples all night. The bottom line is, when bad things happen, focus on the good things surrounding them. It's in the good that you'll find the strength to get through the bad. Bad times come and go, and you've successfully navigated past them before.

Ride The Wave

Pay close attention when things are truly going well in your life, when the money is good, when everything you touch works out as planned, and when your star is shining bright. Do preventative maintenance when you're on a roll and things are flowing better than expected. Don't get caught up in the moment and relax as if you've got it made. Stash away for the next rainy day. Stay on top of things so you can continue to ride the wave.

Be careful not to overlook the small things that have the potential to become big problems. Now that you're achieving your goals, enjoy your moment in time, but don't be careless.

How long will it last? No one but God really knows. Get yourself in a position to survive a fall. Don't be so quick to spend unnecessarily or make new bills until you've taken care of the ones you have. Make sure you help someone else now that you're in a position to do so. Remember, to be blessed, you have to be a blessing.

Celebrate

Each day of life, you have two choices: Make the best of it, enjoying and discovering the many wonderful opportunities another day of living has in store for you, or start the day worried and stressed, which has no positive benefit whatsoever. I suggest you start focusing on the good that can come out of each day. Why not? It's your choice. You choose how your day will go and how you'll let it affect you. What's the right choice each day?

Don't say you don't have anything to celebrate. Snap out of it! Do you have a place to stay? Celebrate! You could be homeless. Don't have a nice car? Celebrate. It may not be what you really want, but at least you have something to get around in. No car? Celebrate! You have legs and the ability to get to the bus or subway. Unhappy at work? Celebrate! You could be unemployed. Lost your job or got laid off? Celebrate! Because you have the skills to get another one, and you will. Live on the positive side of life each day.

Unhappy because your relationship just ended? Celebrate! Now that you have space, take that time to improve on you, and be ready when true love comes your way. And it will. There's a bright side to every difficult situation. You just have to remain optimistic, knowing that this too shall pass. Look around. You have so much to be thankful for, so don't let things get you down. Whatever you're unhappy with won't last forever, so look up toward Heaven and smile.

Soon Enough

Have you met someone new and things just seem too good to be true? Well, you may have finally found the one you're looking for. Be it in your personal life, business, or life in general, there comes a time when you get what you've hoped and prayed for. If you stay the course and keep moving toward what you seek, believing it's there for you, you'll get it.

Maybe you are surrounded by people you don't trust. You're leery of their moves and motives. You just don't feel comfortable around someone who has just recently entered your life. They say the first feelings are the ones you should trust. Or should you? Keep paying attention to their words and actions. Deception can only be sustained for so long before the truth emerges. So hang in there, pay attention every step of the way, because the truth will be revealed.

Sometimes you just have to be patient and wait. Especially once you've run up on a career liar, a career actor, and career manipulator—a person who has run this game over and over, person after person, city after city, time after time. You see, they run it until they get caught, then they disappear to search for another victim to manipulate. Stay cool and pay close attention along the way. You'll discover the truth.

See It Clearly

When your world becomes too noisy, hectic, and out of control, stay focused, be extra calm, peaceful, and patient. Try not to let the circumstances affect the way you feel or cause you to react emotionally without thinking first. Take a minute, and step away from it so you can see what's truly going on. Do something totally different from what you're going through to clear your head. This will allow you to see the situation exactly as it is once you come back to it.

When you act on your emotions, you're more likely to make bad decisions that you'll later regret. On the flip side of things, when you know someone is reacting emotionally to a situation, try not to take it too personally, especially if this behavior reoccurs. Sometimes things are said in anger to pass around the pain. Before you react too quickly, step back, remove yourself from it, and hold your tongue until the emotional fog clears.

If your life in general seems to be swirling out of control, pay close attention to the reasons why and deal with them one by one. Take some time, step away from it, and see it for what it really is. It's very easy to get so wrapped up in a situation that you become the situation you're in. If you don't like what you see or what you're going through, you have the opportunity to change it by changing the way you are. But first you have to step away.

Lighten Up

If you want to live a long, healthy, and happy life, then laugh a lot! Laughter is medicine, and it's within all of us, but you just need to start more of it. Laughter boosts the body's immune system, reduces stress, reduces the risk of heart attack, and even calms you mentally. These are health benefits everyone needs. It's a real tragedy to go through life with a stone face. Too many of us in our quest for success have become convinced that we need to be somber and serious to make it in life. This couldn't be further from the truth.

Ever wonder why you're never asked to go out with your friends? Wonder why your sweetheart stopped suggesting the two of you go anywhere? Although it may not be the only reason, maybe it's because you're too serious. You're just no fun. You have no real sense of humor. Realistically, we all have a sense of humor hidden somewhere. You've just chosen to bury yours for some reason. Maybe it's because of a past pain or the stress you are dealing with every day. You are wearing yourself out—and everyone around you—by being so darn serious all the time. Tell some jokes, act silly sometimes, go to a comedy club or show. Tickle each other. Just do something funny sometimes. Laughter has the power to open many doors of joy in your life. It'll remind the ones who love you why they love you so much if you just laugh sometimes. Life is not that serious all the time.

Give Them Some Time

Children are a precious gift from God. You as a parent are responsible for raising and nurturing that gift. Children can't raise themselves, although some children today are doing just that because their parents aren't around most of the time. To be in the same house and not know what's going on in your child's life is about as bad as not being there. Make a habit of getting into what they're into and finding out what they're thinking. Not only does it help you understand your child's developing personality, it also provides insight into which areas to nurture. Make sure your children are on the right track. Spend time with them.

You make time for work and personal pleasure. Make equal time for your child. If you always drop him or her off with someone else so you can have fun and enjoy life, you're missing out on some very precious years. I know it sometimes wears you out, but they need you. It's never too late to become a part of their lives. If you're having problems and you're wondering why your child is turning out to be a certain way, maybe it's because you haven't been there for him. This doesn't apply to everyone. Some of you are great parents and for that I commend you. You're clearing the path for many blessings in your life by being there for them. But for those of you living life as if you have no children, be very careful. Your child didn't ask to come into this world. Now that you have one, you have a responsibility. So make the best of this wonderful blessing of life. You now have the opportunity to pass on your knowledge, wisdom, and love, giving him or her the necessary tools to be prepared to live life to the fullest. Every chance you get to love, teach and spend time with your children, Jump at it.

Do Something About It

Things happen in life that you have no control over. Simply put, life happens. You can do all you can to be prepared for the unexpected. You can do all you can to make sure things go right and things still go wrong or get out of control. But the good thing about life is you have an inner power. You have power to change things around you, the power to change yourself. Deal with something troubling you, or that "someone out of sync" in your life.

If your relationship is in turmoil, don't ignore it. That only allows the problems to grow deeper. You can't expect your partner to do all the changing and you to do nothing. It takes two working together for change. If you see your children going astray and you don't deal with it, you're enabling that behavior. It may be too late when you finally decide to address it. At the first sign of a problem, deal with it. Act now.

If lack of communication at home is causing your thoughts to venture outside of your family, make it known that you can no longer go on this way before you do something stupid. First pray on it, then talk about it openly. If that doesn't work, seek counseling. Life is too short to allow troubling things that you have the power to deal with or change grow into more than they should. If you don't deal with it now, you'll be forced to deal with it later once it becomes worse. Stop ignoring the problem.

Struggle Builds Strength

Hang in there when things are at their worst. Hang in there when you feel you've done all you can do. Hang in there when there's no one to turn to. These are the times when you must trust and have faith. I know it's easier said than done. And right now, this is the last thing you want to hear. You need help, not advice. But sometimes advice is the best help you can get. If someone bails you out every time you get your back up against the wall, need money, or need help getting through something, you'll never learn to deal with the issues on your own. It's the hard times that make you strong.

If the friend who always comes to your aid is now denying you help, don't be angry with that person. They're only giving you tough love. Trust me. A real friend will hurt as much as you do, knowing they can help you. But it's in your best interest that they don't. Enabling you every time you get into a jam is only keeping you from learning how to cope. Why work at getting better at living life if someone is always there to bail you out so you can make the same mistakes again. Fixing your own problem will make you stronger.

Sometimes you must endure great pain to get to the pleasure. What you avoid doesn't go away. It always comes back to haunt you until the day you finally say enough is enough. Make today that day. Once you deal with your problem on your own and see it through, you'll be able to move on to the next chapter of your destiny. So when those tough times, tears, and pain come your way, stand up and get through it on your own. Don't fear the hard times.

Refuse To Get Caught Up

The next time you get frustrated or upset, refuse to get caught up in it and it will have no power over you. Unexpected problems, small inconveniences, and minor disappointments can lead to major disruptions in your life if you let them. But you have the power not to let them. When you feel frustration coming on, breathe, count to ten, do whatever, but just step back a little bit. Is what you're about to do or say worth it? Is the situation really all that important?

Sometimes you blow the little things way out of proportion. But in reality it's a big waste of time, power, and energy. It doesn't do the situation, you, or anyone around you any good. It only messes up your attitude, destroys your focus, and has a negative impact on your day. Have some guts and start controlling your emotions.

Give the frustrations and problems some distance. When they come into the moment, get away from them for a while. Find a place where you can calmly think things through. If you get into the habit of doing this when tough and difficult moments come your way, you'll find that there's no need to be overcome by frustration. Once you adapt this new way of thinking, your life will progress to a new level of happiness and fulfillment. Don't succumb when negative moments approach.

Let It Go

Stress, frustration, busy schedules, family issues, bills, and un-expected problems have a way of getting the best of you. It'll make you irritable, angry, and even cry. We're all human and that means there's only so much within your power that you can do in any situation. Once you get to the point of having done all you can, move on.

The problems and stress come when you've done all you can in a situation, and you still try to do more. You've given it all you've got, so why are you carrying on about it? You need to step back, be patient, and let the seeds planted from your efforts grow. Know when to push and realize when you now have to wait. But in the waiting process, don't worry about it, because it will work itself out. It always does. Stop pressing the issue.

Things always have a way of working themselves out in time. As the saying goes, "Trying times are but testing times. Times when we must believe in the things we cannot see. Times when we must have faith." So stop pushing an issue that won't budge. If you're trying to make someone love you who has made it perfectly clear they never wanted your kind of love, stop pushing your way into their life. If you're constantly making an effort to be everything to everybody, stop. If you're trying to help someone who refuses your assistance over and over again, stop. Realize that in this life you can only do and give so much. When you've done all you can do and when you feel all hope is gone, fall on your knees, look up, and let it go.

Don't Take Life For Granted

Today was just like any other day. You got up and proceeded through your daily routine of making the world go around. There were people you should have taken the time to say "I love you" to, but you didn't. You were too busy, too tired, too selfish to say three simple words that can move mountains. Maybe you'll do it later. You could've helped the person who called you for assistance during a bad situation. You could have spent time with a relative but never called or stopped by.

You're angry at someone right now and determined not to say "I'm sorry." Why should you apologize? You're too proud to do that even when you know you're wrong. You expect them to get over it. What if there is no later and tomorrow they're gone? How'd you feel knowing you spent the last day of their life missing the opportunity to apologize and show your love? Tomorrow's a maybe. Now is real- ity.

When thirty-three people were senselessly killed at Virginia Tech, they got up on their last morning just like you and me, talking about what they were going to do, planning their week, a vacation, maybe thinking of where to go to lunch in a few hours. They had no idea that this day would be their last. They were assassinated in an instant. I am sure some of them understood the true meaning of life, and some of them, like some of you, just assumed and ex- pected "later" would happen. Understand that each breath is a gift and life itself is a blessing. You have a wonderful opportunity right here, right now.

You're In Charge

Sometimes life gives you the feeling of being in the car but not behind the wheel. It's like you're being driven somewhere you don't want to go. As long as you continue to be the passenger, instead of the driver, you won't decide your destination. When it comes to your life, get behind the wheel.

As long as you allow someone else to decide what comes next along your life's road, you'll keep feeling the way you're feeling, and you'll keep getting what you're getting. You don't have to be unhappy or sad or afraid; you don't have to settle for less than the best in life, unless that's what you choose.

To know this and do nothing about it is living a life of fear. Fear is false evidence appearing real. So why live there? Fear's job is to hold you back. A friend recently sent something to me by e-mail that makes a lot of sense: "Life is ten percent of what happens to me and ninety percent how I react to it." React to your life with joy and a positive purpose, because it affects how your day goes, how your world turns, and what your life becomes. Stop letting life drive you.

Live Life, Don't Let It Live You

Life is a wonderful road in spite of its occasional ups and downs. You just have to decide once and for all to live life and not let life live you. Refuse to let life wear you down. Refuse to fall into depression by hiding your feelings. Refuse to let another day go by without fully enjoying something wonderful. If something is troubling you, deal with it quickly and shed it so you can smile and be happy again. How many days, months or weeks have you been holding back your true feelings about something? By holding it in, you're causing yourself to be in a bad mood, depressed, and unhappy, so let it go so you can exhale and live again. Think of the happiest time in your life. You are in charge of your happiness. Not your husband, wife, boyfriend, girlfriend, family, friends, money, your boss, or even your children. So decide to be happy each day, no matter what.

Do things that really make you happy. The world is a beautiful place, and life is a wonderful journey. So take a walk in the park sometimes, go to the beach, take a trip, socialize with friends, enjoy your home, enjoy your family, pamper yourself, brighten the life of someone who needs a smile, be a blessing to those around you. Refuse to live another day dwelling on what you don't have. Tomorrow is a promise hoped for. The only guaranteed moment you have is now.

Every Day Is A Good Day

Each day we awaken is a blessing, a miracle. The first thing you should say each day you wake up is, "Lord, thank you for another day." If you're in the midst of a difficult time, this may be just what you need to hear. Whatever you're going through, it's just a storm. Storms come and storms go. You've been through them before and as uncomfortable as they can be, you'll make it through this one too. So don't be so down about what's going on right now. Look at the things and people around you that bring joy to your life.

Even if you're in the hospital under intensive care, you're still alive, so it's a good day. If you still have hope in the midst of a difficult time, it's a good day. If you have a roof over your head, a warm place to sleep, a job, your health, and strength—it's a good day. If you have clothes on your back, a car to drive, money in your pocket, a healthy family, your eyesight, your hearing, the ability to speak—it's a good day. Don't make the mistake of focusing only on the problems in your life to the point where you miss out on the little everyday things that are positive. What you're going through is a temporary detour on the road of life. You'll get through this as you have the many tough times before. Don't stress yourself out.

Resist the urge to say "It's a bad day." Instead, say it was a "difficult day." Focus on the good things in your life. Don't feed into your trouble. Don't dwell on the negative. Live life and try again.

You Get What You Pay For

The best in life comes at a cost. Don't expect to have the best if you cut corners. Taking the shortcut can sometimes save you time and money. Sometimes, even if you pay top dollar, it's possible you could experience disappointment, but not likely. You've got to pay the most to have the best.

Paying doesn't mean just monetarily. It also includes paying with your time and effort. In order to move forward and excel, you have to put your heart into it. You will reap what you sow. For instance, if someone you know has nice things and you want the same, then be prepared to do what they did, putting in the same effort to get them. Trouble comes when you put the cart before the horse and get what you want before you can afford it. Then you end up stressing out financially about the very thing you couldn't afford in the first place.

If you aren't giving your best, then the result you're getting is what you'll keep getting. If you buy cheap substitutions, you get substandard quality. If you pay the price for quality things, expect them to last. If you put in the time and make the necessary sacrifices to achieve a goal, expect to achieve it. If you only do what you have to, getting by with no passion for your work, just for the paycheck, expect to be overlooked. The respect you get weighs in equal measure to the respect you give. The best in life comes at a cost.

Take Care Of You

Do you spend the majority of your time taking care of someone or something else? If so, you're taking care of everything each day except yourself. Well, it's time to recharge your life by taking care of yourself first so you'll feel refreshed and invigorated, then you can effectively take care of the other obligations in your daily life. If you look good and feel good, it motivates you to help others. If you take care of your business early in the day, that leaves your mind free to take care of the remaining business involving those around you after the workday is done.

Begin your day by being good to yourself. If you feel good about yourself at the start of the day, the glow you carry with you will be a positive influence on those you come in contact with throughout the day. When you feel good, you do your best. When you do your best, you deliver excellence in all you do. When you deliver excellence, you gain respect and admiration. When you receive that respect and admiration, you feel good about yourself and become eager to do something else great. Anyone can do great things. It all starts with feeling good about you.

Treat yourself to something nice from time to time. Relax. Pamper yourself. Make sure your appearance is together when you step out each day, no matter where you're headed. There's always someone noticing you, and you never know who that may be. If you're good to yourself, you'll be an inspiration to others and make a wonderful difference in the life of those you come in contact with.

Remember Who You Really Are

It's really easy to get so wrapped up in your job, obligations, and day-to-day commitments that you find yourself sidetracked. Life can be so hectic that you fall into a vicious circle of becoming what you do so much so that you forget who you are. If you're not doing the things that really make you happy because of your day-to-day life, it's time you stopped to assess where you are. Are you headed toward your destination or are you stuck somewhere you really never intended to be? If you are stuck in a place or situation that has you unhappy, dissatisfied, and straying from your original plan, then you need to find a way to get back on track right away.

If you keep saying things will get better, but they don't, then make a real effort to change your life into something that pleases and fulfills you. When you moved here, when you got involved in the situation you're in, was that what you really wanted? If it isn't, if you've found yourself living someone else's life, forsaking your original plan, you need to stop this very moment, step out of the picture frame, and look at the portrait of your life at this very moment.

You know how you were raised and what you were taught growing up by your family. You know what you went to school for. You know why you took that position. You had a plan and a goal. Are you still on track? Have you altered your personality so much so that your true friends now find it hard to recognize you? If you've been told you've changed and you're not the same good-natured person that you once were, it's time to check yourself. Life changes, but it doesn't have to negatively change you or kill your dreams. Don't compromise the things you truly desire and believe in. Live on, move on, and dream on.

Expect The Unexpected

Have you been hit with distressing news today? Has something happened recently that shook your world? Are you emotionally upset about something right now? Stop and get a grip on your feelings! Nothing goes right all the time and at any given moment you could be hit with something that comes out of nowhere. It usually happens when everything is going well in your life.

Don't ask me why it happens this way. Life has been operating on the same principles since the beginning of time. When something good happens to you, you're overjoyed, as you should be, but when you're dealing with drama, difficulties, or a crisis, you become upset. That's understandable; but staying in that worried, distressed state of mind only makes matters worse. Calm down, get yourself together, and deal with it. Remember, life is uncertain, so work toward the best it has to offer.

When trouble knocks on your door, do something about it. Don't ignore it—talk to someone to get your frustrations out. But by all means deal with it, or it will deal with you if you do nothing. The quicker you get your thoughts together and strategize a way through the bad stuff, the sooner you can get back to that place of peace you were experiencing before the incident. Life is like the rain. You have a better chance of staying dry if you prepare yourself for a rainy day. The rain will come but it won't last long. It has to end at some time, so enjoy the good times, and be prepared for the bad times.

Be The Best Parent You Can Be

It takes a real man and a real woman to be great parents. Your child could care less about what you have, what you're going through, or what you've been through. In their world, you're just Mom or Dad. A father can set a good example for his daughter by showing respect toward her mother no matter what problems he and his wife may have. If you keep high moral standards as a man, your daughter will expect the same from the man she is with. The same is true of moms.

Show respect toward the father of your children, and sons will more likely act respectful toward others. It's never too late to become a part of your child's life. Whether you're in the home or out, you're needed to teach your son how to be a man and your daughter how to be a woman. Single mothers, never use your children as pawns for a support check, money, or out of anger. Your child has nothing to do with the issues between you and his or her father. If a father is trying to participate in raising the children, isn't rotten to the core, supports them, and has done them no harm, allow him to be a part of their lives. Don't deny him that precious gift. Do your best to always be there for them.

It's Not All About You

Are there people in your life who never get enough? Never get enough of your time and space? Whatever you do for them is never enough? It's always what they want and how they want it? When you suggest something, you always get all the reasons why it won't work or why they don't want to do it, but when it comes to them, they make you feel obligated to always oblige their requests. You find yourself time after time doing what they ask or finding a way to keep them happy, just to keep the peace.

You're making all the sacrifices while they make the demands. They make all the decisions while you just tag along to make them happy.

If they love you as much as they say they do, they'll compromise and meet you halfway at least some of the time. Don't make someone relive your past hurts, problems, and difficulties. Realize that the people who come into your life have needs and desires just as you do. To maintain harmony, you must continually take inventory of your life. If there's someone in your world like this, if you know that person, or if that person is you, look in the mirror.

Be Who You Are And Say What You Really Feel

In this world we live in, so many of us are trying to live up to an image and impress those around us by trying to be more than we really are and appearing to have more than we really have. What people see and think of us is only a mirage. Don't lie about who you are. The truth will come out eventually. Honesty will get you much further than dishonesty in the long run. Eventually, your false claims about what you've done, what you have, who you know, and what you're able to do will come back to haunt you when your hand is called. Agreeing with someone when you feel differently is being dishonest. Rather than agree with something that's wrong, say nothing at all. No one respects a "yes" man or woman, not even the person you're agreeing with, although they won't let you know that. Stop kissing butt to get ahead.

Move Forward

If you feel you're stuck in a rut and not moving forward, it's because you're holding yourself back. No one is forcing you to stay where you are at this point in time in your life. You're where you are because you've chosen to be there. There is something right now, at this very moment, you can do to begin changing your circumstances. You've chosen to blame this lack of progress on something or someone else. Focus on the real problem. The real problem is you.

It's not important why you're in your present state of circumstances. What is important is that you realize you don't have to be where you are and only you have the power to change that. So change it now. Put all of your energy into your desire to change or improve you mental, emotional, financial, and physical conditions. It's time for you to stop feeling the way you do and complaining about how things are.

You can have whatever you want, achieve whatever you set out to, and be whoever you want to be. You may have to change some friends, your attitude, your outlook on life, and step into a new way of thinking, but you can do it. Surround yourself with positive people who've already realized what you're striving toward. Think about it. You're able to do this and have always been able to do this. Stop making excuses and start moving forward.

Put On Some New Clothes

If you're tired of being where you are at this point in your life, change what you're wearing. No one likes wearing the same clothes each day. No one wants to see you wearing the same thing every day. When you put on something new, you look good, you feel good, you get compliments, and you have an outward sense of newness. You're looking sharp. You feel good about yourself. You're clean, pressed, and dressed for success.

Take regular inventory of who you are, where you are, where you're going, and how you're getting there. If your mind and emotions are covered in despair, worry, disappointment, anger, negativity, and bitterness, it's time you go into the dressing room of life to make a change. If you're in the midst of a hurtful situation, there's a time to grieve and a time to let it go and move on. You can't stay there. Stop holding on to the things that have you stuck emotionally, mentally, physically, and spiritually. It's time to take off those soiled, smelly emotions and feelings.

Make up your mind right now to do things differently and look at life through a different window. Get up with a new attitude, go to work with a new glow, handle your business with a new determination. If it's an endless cycle of the same thing. Say no to the way you've been living. What you've been doing has been getting you what you've been getting. If you step up into a newness of life, a new world of happiness and opportunities will open wide.

"When you reach an obstacle, turn it into an opportunity. You have the choice. You can overcome and be a winner, or you can allow it to overcome you and be a loser. The choice is yours and yours alone. Refuse to throw in the towel. Go that extra mile that failures refuse to travel. It is far better to be exhausted from success than to be rested from failure."

~Mary Kay Ash, founder of Mary Kay Cosmetics

Business

As a child, I spent weekends with my grandparents on both sides of my family. I remember riding in a wire basket attached to the front handlebars of my grandfather Hardy Williams Sr.'s bicycle. He and my grandmother lived on a dirt road in Savannah, Georgia. The neighborhood had streets, but not all were paved with concrete. He had a decent car, but on the weekends he enjoyed riding his bicycle, so he'd put me in that basket and we'd ride to the store or just up the road a ways. I enjoyed talking about the things and people we passed along the way.

He was a strong man, a construction worker who built his house brick by brick on the weekends, buying building supplies as finances allowed. He once said to me, "Son, the one thing you have in life that you must always protect is your reputation. Once you ruin it, what you've done will never be forgotten. It may be forgiven but never forgotten."

Your reputation will follow you wherever you go. Tarnish is hard to rub off. You want your reputation to shine. The people you come in contact with will know of you, tell others about you, and respect you before they ever meet you. Your reputation sets the stage for how you're perceived by others.

Once your word is no longer trusted, you may spend a whole lifetime getting back your respect, integrity, and honor. Your word is your bond. Never go back on your word, deal dishonestly, or make promises you can't keep. If one puts faith in you to complete an assignment, see it through and execute it well. Your work, like your word, defines you.

Follow Through

Sometimes in business and life, we take on more than we can bear. Doing what you say you can and will do is very important and an indication of your true character. Before you accept a task or commitment, be prepared to do whatever's necessary to see it through.

That sometimes means personal sacrifices. Realize that. If you can't do something, say so. Biting off more than you can chew just to get ahead can come back to haunt you if you can't meet the deadlines. It's better to say "Let me check my schedule," to buy yourself some time to decide whether you can see the task through, rather than saying "yes" and falling short of the desired goal. Saying "no" when you're asked to take on more of a load can get you more respect that saying "yes" and making a mess of things. Do and accept only what you know you can do effectively or are committed to seeing through, and you'll come way ahead in the end. Having a reputation for being honest will take you to the next level of success.

Stay The Course

When you have a goal to reach, a task or project to complete, it seems everything comes your way to pull you away from it. Family issues, unexpected issues, work issues, relationship issues, or financial issues hit you right when you don't need them. Getting sidetracked leads to frustration. When all sorts of obstacles come your way to keep you from completing a goal or task, stay calm, breathe, address that unexpected event or complication quickly, and then get back on track. Be honest if you're overwhelmed and say so. If an obstacle arises, deal with it quickly. If you can't, set it aside until you complete your objective.

Manage your load and avoid distractions. If your cell phone constantly rings and you don't want to be interrupted, shut the phone off, otherwise the calls will keep coming, sidetracking you over and over again, making the goal more difficult to reach. Put too much food on a plate and you won't be able to eat it all; put too much water in a glass, and the water will spill over. Taking on too many things at once opens the door for costly mistakes. When a goal needs to be met, know when to say "no" and when to say "yes." Manage distractions by avoiding them.

Try Honey Instead Of Vinegar

If things are going awry in your life, your relationships, and your career, your attitude or personality may be the cause. Perhaps you lose your temper easily or get flustered. Try being calmer and kinder. Honey makes food sweeter and pleasant to the taste, and it has many health benefits. Vinegar has health benefits too, but it stinks and tastes bitter. Which would you prefer? Which one are you? Are you the boss that everyone loves because he treats his employees with respect? Or are you the manager that everyone hates because he's mean and uncaring and hard to talk to? If you're the latter, try being sweeter.

Everyone in the office talks about you behind your back because you're mean, self-centered, and selfish. If they stop laughing when you enter the room, avoid you and your office, and stay away from you at company functions, you need to get a grip on things. Sure, you may be having a degree of success doing it your way, but you could really decrease that employee turnover if you stop being so bitter and thoughtless.

Here's how you can begin to change things for the better: Start saying "Thank you" when someone's done something nice, well, or good. Realize that people have lives and families as well as an obligation to your business. They're employees, not slaves.

Fix It And Move On

When things don't come out as you expected, when you make a mistake, what do you do? Do you waste a lot of time and effort covering it up, making up excuses for your mistake, or pretending it didn't happen, hoping no one notices? The mistake will eventually get noticed whether you own up to it or not. Admitting to a mistake softens its consequences and bolsters your reputation. Make life easier on yourself by owning up.

The best thing to do is to simply accept it, admit it, deal with the consequences, and move forward. If you're hiding something on the job or in your personal life that you know was a mistake that could hurt someone or hurt the business you work for, admit to it and deal with it quickly before it does further damage. You'll look a lot better in the end once you've dealt with the problem and solved it right away.

Hush

Are you the kind of person who always talks about what you're going to do? What your plans are? What you're working on, and when it's going to happen before the deal is completed? Do you find that every time you do that, something happens to delay or postpone things? I can't explain it, but I've found that if you keep your peace until the deals are done and completed, in most cases they come off without a hitch. Refrain from sharing your joy before the deal is done.

Be quiet about it. Don't be one of those people always thought of as talking about things that never happen, the person who always has the big deal that never goes through. Will they all go through? No, they won't. But if you hold your peace until they do and talk about your successes after the fact, you'll be perceived as a mover and shaker. So stop putting your foot in your mouth.

My mother always told me to let the work I do speak for me. You don't have to always tell what you're doing or what you've done. If it's good works, it'll be recognized by those who really make a difference. In life, someone is always watching you, and some of those people are jealous and really not your friends. They're just waiting to block your efforts. So be careful what you say about what you're doing and about upcoming plans.

Don't Be Afraid

There are enough things in life to scare you. Horror movies will scare you. Thrill rides can scare you. Facing a fight with a bigger opponent can scare you. I'm here to tell you, you should have nothing to fear. If you must be afraid, be afraid of what fear will do to you. Fear will cause you to miss opportunities, prosperity, love, happiness, the wonders and joys of life. You only live once, so don't fear stepping out into uncharted waters to get to the next level.

The enemy uses fear to keep you away from your destiny. Fear is one of the tools used to keep you from receiving it. Don't let that happen. Don't let fear block your inheritance. Don't let it block you from leaving a bad relationship, making a commitment, leaving past hurts behind, stepping out on your own, going to the doctor, facing your debts, starting a business, or trying something new.

On the other side of fear is a new job. A new life filled with happiness if you commit to your relationship instead of playing the field. You'll have a healthier life if you go to the doctor and face your problems. You'll find a way out of debt if you talk to the bill collectors and work things out instead of ducking and hiding. You'll own a prosperous business if you take the first step and do what's necessary to start it. You'll have a brilliant new career with better pay if you leave the one you now hate instead of complaining about it day after day, making everyone around you miserable. I promise you, if you start believing instead of fearing the unknown, then and only then will the life you should be living begin. Fear is False Evidence Appearing Real.

Open Your Mind

New ideas are born every minute—some good, some bad. Times change. Each day, technology changes. The avenues of information and progress are in a constant state of change. One of the keys to continued success is keeping up with those changes and applying them in the areas where they'll benefit you the most. To be closed to change will keep you stuck where you are. Stay open to progress and new ideas.

In business you've got to stay abreast of new developments in your industry and field of expertise to remain at the top of the food chain. Are you operating your business in the twenty-first century or are you doing things the same way you did them thirty years ago? I'm not saying that the old-fashioned approach should be thrown out the door. No, not at all. Sometimes it's what makes you unique. But if you can add new ideas that make sense to an old- fashioned approach, then don't be afraid to try them.

If the competition is moving way ahead of you, then you need to examine why and make the necessary changes. Face it. They're do-ing something you aren't, and it's beginning to cost you. So instead of drowning in the loss of revenue and keeping your mind closed to new ideas being brought to you, realize that maybe your way could use a little fine tuning. Listen to the ideas of others. Don't feel threat-ened by new approaches or defensive toward those with new ideas. They're not condemning you; they're trying to make you better.

Now Is The Time

If you're employed, don't get upset the next time you're given a task you prefer not to do or one you think is too much to handle. If you accepted it, don't complain about it. Deal with it. If this is becoming more than you bargained for when you took the job, then you need to rethink whether this position is really for you. But before you move hastily, give it a shot, and see what becomes of it. This task may be the one that'll take you to the next level. The time has come to step beyond your comfort zone. Now is the time to explore the unknown.

It may very well be that the profession you're in failed to meet your expectations. If you find yourself regretting each day instead of anticipating the enjoyment in each moment at work, then you must begin moving your sights toward something more fulfilling. If you don't get up each morning with an eagerness to make a difference and excel to the next level on the job, then you're only fooling yourself and wasting the time you should be using to reach your true destiny. Make a move.

Remember, you accepted this job or task. You wanted it, so start being more appreciative of your position. But if you aren't happy where you are, if you're going nowhere with no chance of advancement, be honest with yourself, and stop living a lie. From this point on, begin searching for a career or job that will make you happy. Find a place where you can grow and have a personal sense of fulfillment—a place where you can make a difference.

Be Patient

Are you trying hard to get something accomplished and everything seems to be getting in your way? Have you been working toward a goal only to be set back every time you're close to it? I've been there many times, and I've learned that sometimes it's just not time for you to have it yet. You may still have other things to do to help you prepare for the next position. You will get there if you stay the course. So don't be discouraged.

God knows there is still a lot more you need to have in place before He allows you to get where you're going and have the desires of your heart. Think back on the times when you were upset because things kept going wrong along the way, only to later say after you reached your goal, "I'm glad I went through this to get here." Success takes sacrifice and education to be sustained. Don't be frustrated. If things aren't happening as quickly as you'd like, it's because it's not time for it to happen yet. Rest assured if you stay the course, your moment will come.

Embrace The Challenges

When difficult times come your way, it's normal to be affected by them; but to let them shake up your world only makes matters worse because you're then unable to think things through clearly. Life is a series of reoccurring cycles. If you continue to deal with them the same way each time, and they reoccur, you need to try something new. Otherwise, you're only giving that situation license to repeat itself. Try something different.

No one wants to deal with negatives, but you have to, so embrace them quickly and get to work on solving the issue. Get it behind you. Only you can stop it from becoming more than it really is. If you need to deal with a financial issue, deal with it today. Ignoring it may magnify the obligation and make matters worse. Communicate your situation quickly. Don't run, because it's not going away.

Be it your relationship, children, career, family, or your beliefs, it's important that you always remain in a state of growth. Be willing to move to the next level in every aspect of your life. The only way you'll reach your predetermined place in life, your purpose on this earth, is not to run from things that bring you grief. You'll get through the tough times in life faster and with greater strength if you embrace challenges.

Expect The Best

In every endeavor, in every new situation you choose to be a part of, focus on the positive possibilities. If you focus on and expect the worst, most likely you'll get it because that's what you're keeping an eye out for. You helped create a negative result because you anticipated it happening. Whether you realize it or not, you have the ability to attract confusion, drama, and disappointment to your life, or to repel it with a positive attitude. Life has enough negatives.

Speak positively. Associate yourself with good people. Do positive, happy things. Remove yourself from the company of complaining people who always start a conversation with a problem. They bring you down and will continue to as long as you give them your time. It's okay to say you don't want to hear it. Be honest. Don't worry about how it'll be accepted. Be true to yourself and your feelings. Be honest in every situation you're apprehensive about.

Starting a new job soon? Expect the best. Opening a new business? Expect the best. Moving to a new place, making new friends? Expect the best. Going to the doctor to find out about the unknown? Expect the best. In every situation, as I always say, "It is what it is." So, from this day forth, no matter what those around you may do, look at the bright side of life and every situation with a smile.

Don't Take It Personally

If you go into business with a close friend, you must do it with an open mind. If you value your friendship, it may not be in your best interest to go into business with them at all. But in some instances, it works out very well if the two of you are on the same page. In the event you have differences, understand criticism will come. The question is "Can you deal with it?" There'll be rough roads you'll have to travel and difficult decisions that must be made. Expect all of this. Come to grips with the fact that you may have to hear things that don't sit well with you from time to time. It is business, after all.

You may be upset right now with your partner about something you don't agree with. There's no need to be upset about it. Deal with it. You made the decision to go into this venture. If it's more than you can bear, then get past this and move on. If it's still too much to bear, then maybe it's time you go out on your own. Business is business, not personal.

If your partner manages his finances better than you do and begins to amass wealth while you fail to get ahead financially, don't be jealous or envious. Learn from his or her personal successes as a result of what you've built together. Be happy for your partner. Learn how to better manage your finances. Get to know your banker, maintain and pay closer attention to your retirement plan or investments for the future. The bright side is all may go well for the both of you as you pursue your dreams. On the road to success, if you keep working hard and doing the right thing, your day will come.

Stop Living In Fear

Do you deal with confrontation by avoiding it? Does the very thought or possibility of having a heated conversation scare you? Do you look at opportunities to advance in your career as being too much work or too risky? As long as you live in fear of the unknown, you'll stay where you are in life and continue to get what you've been getting. Your dreams will remain dreams. You'll live your days on this earth wishing for something that will never come if you don't take some chances and expand your knowledge. You're spending so much time fearing what you may not have that you're making problems within what you do have.

You won't apply for that management job because everyone before you failed in that position. You feel you're safer where you are because you've been there so long. You've gotten comfortable and settled for less. Have you ever thought that maybe the position has been waiting for you? That those who failed in that job weren't destined for responsibility? You know why they were fired or moved on. You know and everyone around you knows you can do that job better than anyone else can, but you never go for it out of fear. Deep inside of you, because you're afraid, there's something caged up that's dying to be set free. You know you want and deserve a better life, so go for it!

Understand this: Fear is determined to keep you where you are, stagnant and far from your destiny. Fear is false evidence appearing real. Fear has only as much power as you allow it to have. Stop giving into it. Face it, conquer it, and move forward toward your dream of complete happiness.

Follow Up On Things

When you make a commitment to family, your children, friends, or those you are in business with, it's important that you see it through. If you can't, then don't commit to it. How many things you said you'd do today did you actually do? How many promises and appointments were you really able to keep? In an effort to juggle so many things in life, we sometimes get zealous with our intentions, promising too much and delivering too little. You meant well, but meaning well and doing well are different. If you make a commitment or promise, make sure you follow through.

Worst-case scenario: If you can't do what you said you'd do, then explain why. Don't wait until it's supposed to happen to do it. It's not fair to have someone expecting you to keep your commitment, only to find out after they've rearranged their day that you're not going to make it. Integrity in life is priceless. Protect your reputation. Slow down and think before you commit. When you do commit, give that commitment priority. The only exception is when something comes up that's beyond your control. Start you day right each morning. Don't procrastinate. No one can do it all.

Know your limitations and readjust immediately. Evaluate your priorities. Make promises you know you'll keep. Try not to cram too much into a day. In an effort to bring in as much income as you can each day, you sometimes become overextended, resulting in missed appointments and incomplete work. Don't be greedy. You'll get what's out there for you and more if you keep your word.

Be The Dream

We all have a vision of where we want to go, what we want to be, and how we want to live our lives. If you're working your way toward it, that's wonderful. If not, then get started now toward your destiny; but you have to do more than just move toward a dream, you have to become it. You must adapt the lifestyle in your mind. Become it in your thoughts, your actions, and in the way you approach life. If you don't know how, then find out how to become the dream you desire for your life, and put the knowledge you acquire into practice. Just be careful in the process that you don't lose sight of who you really are.

Think the part, dress the part, act the part. Learn your craft. In becoming your dream, you'll also have to do some closet cleaning. Ask yourself what and who contributes to your positive outlook and the pursuit of your dream. A good friend supports you along the way with encouragement and assistance by being understanding and happy for you. If you have people in your life who hold you back from what you have your sights set upon, then you must make a decision. Allow them to keep you off track or cut them loose. If you allow others to steer you, you'll never arrive at your dream.

Someone else's uncertainty about your dream shouldn't matter. Cancel some associations and head toward your destiny without them. They may not understand why, but if they really love you, they'll be there for you when you arrive.

Get It Together

Are your voicemail and answering machine full? Do you have a cut-off notice, not because you don't have the money, but because you haven't opened the mail in over a week? Does your child have to remind you that the two of you were supposed to do something today? Did you forget because you were so overwhelmed and busy? Now you're trying to find out how to fulfill your commitment in the midst of a day that's already overbooked with too much on your plate. You're either eating too much or never taking the time out to have a decent meal. As for sleep, if you get five continuous hours in once a week, you're lucky. That's if you can sleep that long. Why are you living in such chaos?

It's the little things that make a big difference if neglected too long. It's the little things that flavor your character and provide the molding around your reputation. So if any of this applies to you, take some time to sort it all out, away from work and stress, and do it soon.

If you need to get organized and prioritize, get to it so you can relax a bit more. I've got a news flash for you: The merry-go-round of this world will continue to turn if you get off every once in a while to smell the roses. Take the time to smell the roses of life before they wither and die.

Accept Responsibility

Running from problems and difficulties says a lot about your character. For instance, if you go into a joint venture that goes sour, the two of you should share the responsibility of the outcome. It's wrong to run and hide, leaving your friend, partner, or family holding the bag when you know you were part of the situation. Using people is wrong and believe me, it will come back to haunt you. A coward runs from responsibilities. If you're wrong or at fault in any situation, don't be weak avoiding the issue.

It's not always a pleasant thing to do. Sure, admitting you were wrong when things don't work out as planned is something you'd rather avoid, but that's the cost you sometimes pay as you travel life's road when it comes to business. Don't expect to always achieve success the first time around. Those shortfalls will build a solid foundation for future opportunities. Be it because of poor planning, lack of information, bad judgment, ill intentions or just plain bad timing, sometimes things fail to work because it just wasn't the appointed time for it to happen. Stop running from problems and take responsibility. Why is maintaining your integrity so important? The only thing you really have to sustain you in life, whether you're successful, is your reputation. Once that's tarnished, the stain is hard to wash out. Confront the issues in your life, be they good or bad, and you'll be able to get up and try again with the respect of those around you because you were honest and up front. It may be uncomfortable to fess up to the truth, but you'll come out a winner if you do.

Pay Attention To The Details

Rushing through what you need to take care of could cause you problems later on, so slow down. Pace yourself. Outline tomorrow's duties today so you'll have a road map to follow. You wouldn't take a road trip without a map or a navigation system, would you? We often spend too much time fixing problems and not enough time avoiding them. Get it right the first time. When you feel you've finished something, before you move on to the next thing ask yourself, "Is it really complete?" Review what you've done carefully and go over each point or item to make sure it's what you intend it to be. It may not be correct or right all the time, even if you give it your best, but you can rest each night knowing you tried. So before you consider something done, check, recheck, go over it all.

It's the little things you didn't give the proper attention that tend to cause the problems. Will you come out perfect even after you've paid attention to the little things? Not always, but you'll come out much better than if you rushed through it. Maybe you have too much on your plate. If so, don't be afraid to delegate some of your smaller tasks to someone else. Sometimes you have no choice but to hurry. It happens even if you try your best to get started early on something. But even when rushed, give special attention to details. If you can't do it, if it's too much to handle, then say so. Don't let someone else's demands upon you cause you to give less than your best. If you need more time to give the best you've got, then say so. If it's undone and full of mistakes, it's a bad reflection on you. A reflection you don't want to see in the mirror of your life. So pace yourself, prioritize your time, and take it slow.

Stop Defeating Yourself

How many times have you worked your way to a point only to do something that takes you right back where you started? It happens from time to time unintentionally, but sometimes you repeat the same mistakes over and over again because you refuse to listen to reason or open your eyes to new ways to complete what you started and reach your destination. If you fail to take the time to analyze the reason for your mistake, there's a good chance you'll repeat it.

If you set out to do something and you have a negative attitude going into it, expect problems because you're bringing them with you. Why do it if you're going to concentrate on the reasons why it won't work? Looking at the pros and cons of a situation is one thing, but shooting down every idea that comes up in discussion is destructive.

If you're going to be negative about everything that comes up, if you don't believe in it, then why are you involved? If you have someone like that on your team or in your life, get rid of them. If you're that person, you're only hurting yourself.

Wonder why no one calls you to be a part of their activities or projects? It's because they don't want to deal with your attitude. Stop being a liability to yourself and others. There is a bright side to every situation, and you need to realize that. It's time to move forward with a positive attitude.

If You Seek It

If you really desire to achieve a goal when you are in business, you must do what's necessary to establish yourself as a serious contender. Layer your organization with the best equipment, the most talented and best people, the best technology, and experienced, knowledgeable partners, and management you can trust and depend on. Surround yourself with individuals with the same determination and drive you possess. Working together, if your business or company is truly determined to attain a reputation of being the best, you'll get there.

Yours is among many that have set out with that same goal, only to allow life to get in the way. Personal problems, financial issues, family situations, greed, power struggles, sabotage, envy, and cracks in one's business can taint the entire project, process, and company. Work with your weakest link. Developing a good business reputation is priceless. Once you get there, don't mess it up for yourself. Refuse to allow anyone or anything to tarnish you or your business. A good reputation will take you anywhere. Screw it up, and you will never be seen the same. Whatever went wrong may be forgiven but never forgotten. Being known for operating with an excellent work ethic, integrity, and constantly striving for perfection is something that requires time, personal sacrifice, and hard work. Stay focused.

If You Have The Job, Do Your Job Or Quit

If you have a job, but a bad attitude about it, you need a wakeup call. Realize there is someone else out there who wants and will appreciate having your position. Someone who could probably do the job much better than you or at the very least will try harder than you with more passion and appreciation. When you accepted your position, you agreed to give it your best, so do your best, no matter what you may feel otherwise. Good, secure, decent-paying jobs are hard to find.

If you have a less than positive attitude about what you do, then you really should leave. It's not right, fair, funny, or acceptable for you to do as little as you can each day just to get a paycheck. Stop complaining about what you do, who you work for, and the conditions you're working under. Instead, be diplomatic. Leave your personal problems at home. Smile when you greet your clients. Drop the gossip on the job and keep your personal affairs to yourself. Stop putting your work off on someone else or a co-worker who has their own work to do. Treat your customers with respect and honor. Make each one of them feel like you're happy to see them. Get to work on time. Better still, get there a little early.

You weren't hired to just get by to get paid. You were hired to make a positive difference and to help the company flourish. Give that opportunity to someone else if you don't like it or want it before it's taken away from you, because eventually it will be taken away if you keep performing poorly and with a bad attitude. Don't think for one minute it's not being noticed. You can be replaced. The way you carry yourself and how you perform are a reflection on who you are, so do your best every day or move on.

Teamwork Makes The Dream Work

If you work, are employed, own a business, are on a committee or are sharing a responsibility with more than one person, this message is for you. Unless you work alone, you have people you have to coordinate with to get things done. You can't just do what you want each day with no regard for the proper order of things necessary for the business or project to work. If you want to do your own thing, and you don't want to work in sync with those around you, then find another job or start your own business. Just get out of the way. Everyone has to be on the same page to get the task done. If you always find reasons why it can't happen, if you look at how hard things are instead of finding a way to get it done regardless of the difficulty, you'll always have problems fitting into a worthwhile work environment. If you're going in a different direction, if you get to work late, if you don't give it your very best every day, if everyone's advancing except you, you're not really a part of the team. In order for a football team to win, everyone has to hold and handle their position once the ball is in motion and the play begins. When all things are in harmony, and the play is executed perfectly, you score a touchdown. But if a player doesn't follow the play pattern, yardage could be loss, the ball could be intercepted, or the quarterback may get sacked.

In the workplace, when you don't do your job to the best of your ability, it ripples through the organization and leads to lost time and frustration. The same applies to your family, relationships, and personal life. You can't do your own thing or slack off while the rest of the family is working together. You can't keep spending while your partner is trying to save. If you have a dream, an ultimate goal in business, love or life, talk about it and get your family and co-workers aligned. Become a serious part of the team so you can share in the group's success.

"If you can somehow think and dream of success in
small steps, every time you make a step,
every time you accomplish a small goal,
it gives you confidence to go on from there."

— John H. Johnson,
founder of the Johnson Publishing Company

Success

I come from a strong, proud but modest family of survivors. We stand together when things fall around us, not only because we were taught to, but because we had to. When I started out in radio in Savannah during high school, I wanted to be the very best announcer on the air. It didn't matter if I was the best in the world; I just wanted to be the best where I was so I could be happy with me.

Being creative and a leader all of my life—starting from high school, where I was senior class president, to this present day—I always reached for something bigger and better. I always sought to start something new, which resulted in three television shows, articles, songs, opening a nightclub, record producing, managing artists, and performing voiceover work worldwide.

I was taught by my family that I had only one shot at this thing called life, so I strive to be the best at whatever I do, or I just don't do it. But most of all, whatever you do, if it's in your heart, no matter what the difficulties may be along the way, don't give up. Failure is not an option. Success belongs to all of us. You just have to embrace and claim it for yourself.

Change Your Way Of Thinking

Your power and success in life is limited by only one thing: your way of thinking. When you're worried, negative, expect the worst, or are discouraged, it shows a lack of faith. This air of self-doubt is nothing new. All of us have been guilty of it at some point along life's road. Stop it! Stop thinking about the worst that can happen and concentrate on the best that can arise from a bad situation. Stir up your faith today and get out of that rut. If you expect the worst, one way or another it'll find you every time.

Expect the best, and it too will find and be drawn to you. It's time you stop thinking about what you can't do and start thinking about what you can do. Are you unhappy at work? Have you had enough? Then find a new job where you can feel happy, fulfilled, and start taking steps to get there. Are things constantly out of order at home? What can you do to make things better? Have you got bills that need to be paid and not enough money to do it? Think of ways to get it done, call your creditors and buy yourself some time until you can get them paid. Stop putting yourself in that same situation over and over again by buying things you know you can't afford. Before you can change yourself, you've got to change your way of thinking. Thoughts are just thoughts until you put them into action. Harness the power within you.

See It Coming

Life gives us so many chances and success is yours. Just keep your mind clear enough to see it coming. You can make it through successfully each day of the year. Each day you get the job done is a day of victory. To achieve success you have to believe it with all that's within you. Increase your knowledge every day and enlarge your vision. Each day, take another step up. Don't let anyone hold you back; but in order for this to happen, the seed has to take root in your heart. Before you're ever going to be successful, you've got to see yourself being successful. Before your dreams come to pass, you've got to look through your eyes of faith and see them come to pass.

People stuck in a rut and those unhappy with their lives do not want to see others succeed. Don't allow them to distract your heart and the vision of your dream. Complete what you've started, no matter what. Avoid the negative and distracting people, situations, and things that are holding you back. Some must work themselves out, some you have to learn to just ignore and walk away from, and some you just have to move out of the way. Did I say it was easy? No. But you have to stay focused on your goal. You've got to stay positive to defeat the negativity in your life. Visualize success. Live it. Be it. Do it. Enjoy it. Constantly meditate on it. Before long, you'll begin to see the dreams God placed in your heart come to pass.

Don't Give Up

You have been and will be provided many opportunities to advance in life. Be prepared by constantly learning and growing. Are you afraid to step out and take the opportunity sitting before you because you aren't sure it's the right thing to do? Has your life become stagnant and mediocre because you're afraid to try new things? In order to experience the abundant life in store for you, you have to start moving forward and explore the open doors in your path. If there aren't any open doors before you, find one, make one, and open it. Open it by making a contact, phone call, or walking up and making yourself known.

The negative forces surrounding you and within you will trap you in a cage of mediocrity, and sometimes you fall for it. Once you start moving forward, nothing can stop you. You may encounter some closed doors before you find the open doors, but if you keep moving, you'll be one step closer to fulfilling the plan of success and victory chosen for your life.

You know how good you are when you're on a roll. Stay focused! Don't ever let a business associate, wife, friend, lover, manager, husband, girlfriend, supervisor, boyfriend, or family member hijack your drive and determination. Don't Give Up! Stop concentrating on what's wrong and build on what's right about your life. Once you make the decision to fully use the abilities and resources you have at your disposal, you'll reach your destiny and enjoy the wonderful life in store for you.

Make That First Step

Do you always play it safe? Are you avoiding a risk or opportunity because you're afraid you might fail? It's okay to be afraid, but being afraid will never get you past where you are right now. Your circle will never grow, your finances will stagnate, and you'll never reach your full potential.

Do you feel that what you're dreaming of may be too difficult? Trust yourself enough to step out on faith. You may not always know what will happen. What you're striving for may or may not come to fruition. Sometimes you'll be afraid, and you may not feel qualified. But you owe it to yourself to try. Stop thinking about it and talking about what you're going to do. Nothing will happen for you if you don't take action.

Whether you have faith or not, the Book of Joshua says, "Don't be afraid. Be strong. Be bold. Be very courageous for the Lord your God is with you wherever you go." The next time you know an opportunity is crossing your path, step out of your comfort zone. Step out in faith. The best is around the corner. It's already yours. It's just waiting on you to arrive. Be willing to take some risks and only then will you achieve your goals, climb the ladder of success, and realize your dreams. When you look back on it all, you'll realize it really wasn't as hard to do as you made it out to be.

Burn Some Bridges

We've all heard "Never burn a bridge, because you don't know when you'll have to go back across it." I disagree with that notion. There comes a time when you have to burn some bridges, a time when you realize you never want to go back across to the other side because there's nothing left over there for you but frustration, depression, pain, unhappiness, and problems.

If you're dependent on an abusive mate, if you're afraid of him or her and you feel you can't make it without that person, leave that sick son-of-a-demon and move on with your life. You can make it through the storm into the sunshine without fear, without the pain.

Have you had it with your abusive boss or that dead-end job with no chance for advancement? If your working conditions are less than adequate, if your skills are never recognized but used over and over to advance the company with someone else always getting the rewards, use what you've learned from these situations to start looking for another job. Never be a slave to a paycheck.

If you're trying to kick an alcohol or drug habit, but every time you get a little clean time under your belt your supplier or your drug friends show up on your doorstep to party, shut the door. Better still, don't answer it. Change your phone number. Don't talk to them anymore. If they leave a message, don't return the calls. You can't get clean if you keep swimming in dirty water.

If you never burn a bridge, you'll be stuck with old, broken-down bridges, leaving you no room to build new ones in your life—new bridges to bigger and better places. So from this day forth, get some fire up under you. Take charge of your life. Have faith and stay firm in your convictions. Take a step in a new direction and stick to it.

Don't Fail Before You Try

Ever talk yourself out of an opportunity before you even gave it a try? Something good comes your way and instead of figuring out ways to make it happen, you figure out the reasons why it won't. How many opportunities have you wasted by looking at the reasons why you can't do something, instead of focusing on how you can?

Maybe you're in a rut mentally because of a number of disappointments resulting from projects that, for whatever the reason, didn't pan out. Instead of giving negativity power, use that energy positively to get past those obstacles the next time a good situation presents itself. Use lessons learned to work in your favor the next time opportunity comes knocking.

Stop being disappointed about things that aren't meant to be yours. Ever think about the fact that maybe God doesn't want you to have that right now. Or better still, maybe you think you're ready for it but He knows you're not. If you are ready, don't be afraid. Go for it! Take this opportunity now. Take the step up to the next level of success and concentrate only on how you can make it happen, not on why it can't. Make a vow to stop doing this to yourself.

Don't Let The Rearview Stop You

When you're driving do you constantly look in the rearview mirror or do you keep your eye on the road ahead of you? Too many people today spend their days looking in the rearview mirror of their lives. Focusing on the past keeps you from moving forward. You don't have to deny that painful things have happened to you. If you've lost a job, been mistreated, or had a loved one die, those are real hurts; but in order to move forward with your life, your feelings, and your dreams, you have to leave the past behind you, look forward, and move on.

Don't carry those disappointments around with you. Stop believing nothing good could possibly happen today because of what happened yesterday. Let go of shattered dreams and broken promises. Stop carrying that ball and chain of pain around your neck. Stop letting it rise up like a mad dog only to cause more pain. Stop dwelling on the disappointments, and forgive the people who have hurt you. Don't just say it. Mean it! Really forgive them.

Release all that bitterness. To reach your destination you have to look at what's ahead, not what's behind you. God never said life would be easy, but He gave us a chance to live it with a purpose. Decide right now to let the past go.

Take The First Step

The first step in moving forward into a fresh future is forgetting yesterday's failures, hurts, and disappointments. No matter what people have done to you, or how unfair life has been, you'll come out stronger than before if you leave the past behind. It's over; it's history; stop living it over and over each day. Learn from it and move toward a more positive lifestyle.

Don't quit believing in your dreams and goals just because times are tough right now. Refuse to let someone else discourage you. Tough times are but trying times, times when we must have faith.

Don't ever think good things won't happen for you. They will. Hardships, difficulties, and trials are the building blocks for the next level of success if you learn from them. If you want a more positive and productive life, then act like it's already happening. Stand up straight, hold your head high, walk tall, speak positive words of life, and you'll be able to feel the difference it makes. Whatever struggles you're going through right now, no matter how large or small they may be, although things may not look so bright in your life today, it's all subject to change if you believe it will. Stop talking about how bad it is and giving depressing issues power. Success is yours if you believe it's yours.

Be Prepared

Are you ready when the meeting starts? When the show begins? When it's time to deliver the goods? When do you meet deadlines? Would you choose going home and getting tomorrow's presentation ready, or going out for drinks after work with co-workers? Skip the cocktails. Some people can handle both and some can't. Work tomorrow doesn't mean just getting by. You were given the job, you accepted it, so do the job. Keep your priorities in the right places. Stay focused!

If you have something due tomorrow, then check, and double-check your work tonight. Over time, being unprepared will show that you haven't given your best effort. Take inventory of yourself. Make sure everything's ready when it's your time to shine.

If you run a store, make sure you're ready to open before you open. If you need to get to work early, then get there early. Ask your boss for an evaluation instead of waiting for one. Go into your manager's office tomorrow and ask for a critique of your work. A good supervisor will be impressed with you for taking that initiative. They'll say, "Now there's someone who wants to improve their performance and move up in the company." Respect your position. Do your work better than your best.

Don't Let It Break You Before Your Breakthrough

It feels good when things are going well. You're on top of the world. You look and feel great. Nothing can go wrong that you can't handle. When things are going bad it causes pain, mental anguish, physical distress, setbacks, and emotional breakdowns. You question your direction and purpose and ask yourself, "Why Me? Why now?" If you're not careful, the whys of worry will snatch you down to a place you never planned to be.

Sure, you feel like there's no way out, but understand that we all must face tests in this life. You must face a test of your determination, a test of your emotions, a test of your character, a test of your strength, a test of your abilities, and most of all, a test of your faith. If you don't know where your true strength lies, re-examine where your life is going. Seek and you shall find that strength to carry on when you feel all hope is gone. Hope is never really gone. You have to find it. Just because you may be in a dark place right now doesn't mean there isn't light ahead. Know who you are and where you're headed and you'll find the light.

Negative forces try to break you because they see the blessing that's coming your way. Before you're about to reach the finish line, negativity is at work to make sure something gets in the way. You have two choices: be defeated or win the fight. Be a winner. Fight your way through this to your blessing.

Don't Talk About It, Do It

Are you the person who always talks about what you're going to do, but always slow about doing it? You habitually put things off for one reason or another. You dread getting started. You're afraid because you feel you don't know enough. The unknown is one of the hardest things to face and overcome. The key is to start facing your fears instead of avoiding them. Instead of spending time with the TV or doing something else to get your mind off what needs to be done, get started on it because the task is not going away. Procrastinating compounds problems, which can pile up and eventually overwhelm you. Deal with problems now and tomorrow they will be behind you.

Want to impress someone in your life or in your company? If asked about it, keep your conversation short and brief until your task is completed. Got things piling up around the house, mail stacking up, issues that need addressing? Stop saying, "I need to get to this" and never doing so. Go through it. Deal with it. Get it done and behind you. The more you put off personally or professionally today, the more you'll have to do tomorrow.

Slow Down

If you're fenced in, overwhelmed, and stressed out, maybe you're taking on more than you can handle. Even if you're capable of completing the task, it may not be the best thing for you to do if your plate is already full. Why? Because if you're already overloaded, you're setting yourself up to make mistakes.

No one can do it all. And no one who has ever become successful or prosperous has done so without the help of others somewhere along the way. Delegate some responsibility if you have to meet a close deadline. Give the people working around you an opportunity to help out. If that's not possible, and you must do it, then pace yourself. Don't agree to unrealistic deadlines. Take your time. Remember when you were in school, how you'd go over your paper before turning it in? Leave enough time to make sure it's right.

If you continue to take on more than you can bear and it's unraveling your world, then consider doing something else more fulfilling, less stressful, and less demanding. If you seldom have time to spend with your family, take a vacation, nurture your children, enjoy a good laugh, or just look at the clouds from time to time.

Take Responsibility

When something goes wrong in your life, is it always someone else's fault? Do you point a finger at everyone but yourself? You started the argument, you lied, you made the mistake. No one on this earth is perfect. It's okay to make a mistake. But it shows a lot of character when you admit you're wrong. The moment you stop blaming your misery on others, it disappears.

Insisting you're right when you're really wrong sustains arguments, anger, and causes divides in associations and relationships. Some will tolerate your lack of responsibility for your actions and others will just disappear. Life's too short to deal with someone who thinks they're always right and blameless. The moment you take responsibility for your life, you jump into a new level of effectiveness and achievement.

Has your blaming, fighting, running, hiding, and avoiding the truth ever brought you anything of real value? No, it hasn't and it never will. Saying you're sorry and admitting you're wrong causes you to grow, opens up avenues of communication, and dissolves irreconcilable differences. It can save your job, your family, your marriage, and friendships. It relieves pressure and allows you to move on to a beautiful, overwhelming abundance of positive possibilities.

Enjoy Each Day Like It's Your Last

We often get so caught up in the day that we forget to live today to the fullest. We put too much trust in tomorrow. Don't take today for granted. What could you have done today that you had the time to do, but didn't? Why didn't you, if you could have? It's a new year. Take advantage of this opportunity to treat life with a little more respect. Today is another chance to get it right.

If you mistreat someone and you don't apologize before the sun goes down, you could live to regret it tomorrow. That person may not be around to receive your apology. If you can see or experience something new today, do so. If you can talk to a family member you haven't spoken to because of stubbornness or resentment over something in the past that's hurt your feelings, pick up the phone, make a call to talk it out. Get past it so you can finally be free of those feelings.

Stop walking around with a chip on your shoulder because someone has hurt or offended you. Stop living in a state of fear. Stop talking about traveling. Do it! Stop thinking about expanding your business. Do it! Stop wishing you had time make time. Do what you feel! Stop making yourself miserable. Choose to be happy from this day forth. If it means eliminating some people from your life, do it! Go after what you want with passion. Each day, make it one step closer to your dream.

Keep Trying

You've been trying and trying, giving it all you've got, but now you're feeling you just can't make it happen, so you're about to give up. Don't do it. Don't stop now because you're almost there. There's a reason for the delay. There's a reason why it's taking so long. You'll realize why once you get there. Just don't give up. You've put too much into it. If you have been hearing "no" from everyone you talk to, if it's causing you harm, hurting you, and leaving scars everywhere you turn, then maybe you should examine whether this goal you're after is the proper one for you to pursue; but if you have the expertise, if you have the knowledge, if you know the situation well, then stand strong and hold on to your dream. People around you may call you crazy. Those closest to you may be doing everything in their power to discourage you. Realize that you are not alone. Every successful person who has achieved their dream has come to a fork in the road. They pushed on past the discouragement, and their dreams became reality. If you have good intentions, go for it. This goal is yours. This desire is yours. The passion for it is yours. If what you're doing to get there isn't working, then try something else. If you've hit a brick wall, find a way over, through, or around it. Find a new way to make it work. Knock on another door. Try something else. You've come too far to quit now. If you believe in what you're pursuing, then refuse to fail. Make it happen. You can do it, and you will achieve it if you believe in yourself. Don't let it break you before your breakthrough.

Yes, You Can

At the beginning of the year you set some goals. Are you still on track? If not, what happened? Why'd you let it erode your drive and determination? This is the year to finish what you started and accomplish your vision. Once you take the first step forward, each additional step gets easier. So stop saying you can't do it.

Been thinking of going back to school, but you keep finding reasons to wait? Maybe you're afraid you may not be able to get that scholarship or a loan, that you won't be able to make the time in your daily schedule. Success takes sacrifice. There are so many options available to you today that will allow you to go back to school. So stop standing on the word "can't." Stuck in a situation because you've convinced yourself or been told you can't make it out here alone? There are free programs and good people to help you and ways to achieve whatever you desire in life if you just seek them out. The only thing holding you back in this world is you. Get mad about being stuck where you are.

Stop expecting support and encouragement from those around you. Break out of your funk right now! Don't just dream about it. Achieve it. This moment is the beginning of the rest of your life. Put your mind to it and do it.

Keep Pushing

Sometimes when you give something your all and you try as hard as you can, you still fall short of your goal. That's when you have to reach deep inside. There are powers within all of us called will and faith. When you put those together, you find a reserve of strength. When you think you've done all you can do, when you feel you can't make it any further, when it seems all hope is gone, draw upon that strength.

Do you have a dream you're pursuing without the support of those around you? Don't let accomplishing your goal hinge on who does or doesn't support you, even if it's the one you love with all your heart. You came into this world alone, and you'll leave the same way. Based on that premise, sometimes you have to strive toward your dream alone. Don't be discouraged when you hear negative comments. Follow what your heart says to do. Pursue your destiny.

All of us have a specific purpose in life. Once you find yours, go after it like your life depends on it, because it does. That purpose is your life, and you can achieve that dream if you stay focused on it and not the negative responses you get. No matter what your age or status, you can still accomplish your dream. It's never too late. In the end, some of the very people who discouraged you will be your biggest supporters. They just can't see what you see right now, so don't worry about them.

Learn From Your Mistakes

The next time you do something wrong, don't be so hard on yourself. Of course you never want to be wrong. No one does. Accept the fact that as you live, you will make mistakes from time to time. Some come from not being prepared. Some come from being hardheaded and refusing to listen. As a result, you find out the hard way you were wrong and what someone was trying to tell you was right. Mistakes remind us we don't know it all. As you live, there's always more to learn. There's more to learn about your relationship, a project, your job, your loved ones, and most importantly, yourself. Learn from the things you have said or done wrong. Our mistakes can be building blocks to better outcomes. Mistakes keep you on track. When you make one, take time to think about why it happened. Then do what you must to make sure you don't make that mistake again. If you don't take the time to think about your errors, you'll repeat them. A mistake means you're making progress. It means you're putting forth effort. Don't be afraid of falling short. With each mistake you learn something more to make you better.

Success comes from not avoiding the possibility of mistakes, but from finding a way to move forward in spite of them. So instead of being depressed, discouraged, angry, dejected, embarrassed, or beating yourself up, get over it. Embrace the wisdom it's left with you and move forward knowing you don't have to travel that path again.

Do Your Part To Make It Happen

Dreams are a wonderful thing. They inspire us to work hard toward a goal, or at least they should. If you really want to achieve your dream, you have to stop talking about it and put some work in toward it. Each day, do something constructive toward making it a reality. That's the only way you'll achieve it. Don't let what you must do to make your world go around keep you from taking positive steps daily toward your dream. You'll see it materialize if you're willing to make sacrifices and put in the time.

The beauty of making strides toward your goal is that with each step closer, you build momentum. With each step, you build confidence. You begin to know that you will achieve your dream. Spend more time walking toward it instead of sitting in front of the television. You've got to strive toward your dream because it is not going to come to you.

Take a course, attend seminars, read books, consult with those living a similar existence associated with your dream. You may have to change your lifestyle, eliminate some associations, or change some bad habits. You'll have to discipline yourself. You have to become it inside. Live as if you're already there. A dream will remain a dream unless you move toward it.

Observe Those Around You

In your office, on your job, in your church, in your neighborhood, in your club, in your circle of friends or in your family, there is someone successful who can teach you something if you observe the way they move about life. If you don't feel comfortable asking for their assistance along the road, watch their moves. If they keep advancing in life and you're not, just pay attention. Successful people are that way for a reason.

If you've been blindsided by something recently, maybe it's because you've been too wrapped up in your world to realize what was happening around you. I'm not saying you need to gossip or stay in everyone's business, but you must stay aware of what's going on around you. That's the only way you'll be able to see what's coming. If you see dark clouds, you know a storm's coming. Birds know when it's time to leave for the winter. They follow the signs of the season. If good people are leaving your workplace like it's on fire, then you need to find out why, and adjust your life accordingly. Things happen for a reason, and you should know why.

You can sense danger, avoid confusion and arguments, make the right career moves, make the proper decisions, move ahead in your career, and avoid the traps if you slow down and pay attention. If you don't know the right path to take, closely watch the moves of those who are well on their way to where you want to go, and you'll find the keys to getting there.

See The Big Picture

Are you the person who doesn't want to hear what's going on, but you always complain about the way things are? You never understand why some things happen because you don't want to know the reason why. You refuse to face the fact that you may be the cause of some of the problems. If it points toward you, do you always point the finger back? Are you convinced your life is messed up because of someone else's actions when in reality you're as much a part of the problem as they are? Up to this very moment, someone's been trying to help you understand beyond what you comprehend. It's time you see the world around you.

If you take a moment and accept the fact that maybe you, the only perfect person in this world, could be wrong, you may learn something about yourself and the things you thought you were upset about. Look at yourself in the mirror. You're complete. You're the one with all the answers. Then why is your life in a constant state of confusion? Why are you always depressed when those around you are happy in spite of life's ups and downs? There's more to whatever has you unhappy, angry, frustrated, or upset.

You're about to be in this thing called life alone because you're so stuck on your way of thinking. Eventually, those who are trying to help you will give up on you and move on if you don't wake up to the world around you. If you keep doing what you're doing, you'll keep getting what you're getting.

Are you tired of the same old routine? Do you often complain you're tired of things, yet you do nothing to move past your situation? Complaining about your life will get you nowhere. Complaining is redundant, senseless, and annoying. Others are sick of hearing you whine. If you've been in the same situation so long that you've become comfortable and afraid to change, stop bellyaching about it. If you don't like it, then do something about it! If you say you want to do something different, then do it.

In order to have something better than what you now have in life, you have to do something better to get it. Improve yourself, learn more, step out of your realm of understanding and onto another level. If you pursue the things necessary to invite change and reach your goals in life, you'll never get there. So stop saying you're going to take a class; stop saying you're going to move; stop saying you're going back to school; stop saying you're going to get a better job; stop saying you're going to get out of that bad relationship; stop saying you're going to clean and organize your house; stop saying you're going to give up your habit; stop saying you're going to change. You've been saying it so long, people around you have stopped listening. It's now become idle chatter. It's time to take action toward change for the better in your life.

Stop Chasing Rainbows In The Dark

If you really want something, you have to take action and do something to get it. It's not going to happen based on just thoughts and desires. You've got to physically put your life in motion toward your destination. Talking about it won't do it. Dreaming about it won't do it. Waiting on God to bless you with it without effort on your part is a senseless quest toward something you'll never attain. It's like saying I want a new car but you haven't saved a dime or prepared your credit so you can get it.

If you want that new job, prepare yourself for it. If you want a new career, research the qualifications. Go back to school if you have to and get qualified. If you want a new home, then get yourself in a solid financial position. If want nice things, but you can't get them because your credit's jacked up, get it straight. Change your living habits, stop buying things you don't need, and discipline yourself. Appreciate and enjoy what you already have. You don't have to have everything you want right now. That's what got you in debt in the first place.

If you're buying things you can't afford because you want it now, sure you've got it going on, but your income-to-debt ratio is too high, and you're shelling out more each month than you're bringing in. Now your nights are sleepless. All you do is work to pay for it all, and you're dodging the bill collectors. You wanted it, so face the music.

Wake up! Life takes its own course, but you've got to do the driving if you want to get to your destination. Success and happiness do not just come to you. You have to make your way toward them if you plan on achieving them. It's time you got sick and tired of being sick and tired. So stop thinking about it, stop talking about it, do something about it. Hit the switch. Turn the lights on.

Leave Your Comfort Zone

In order to take yourself to another level of happiness, in order to arrive at the next level of success and prosperity, you must be willing to and eager to change, to learn something new, to try something different, to open the door to the unknown. If you stay where you are and keep doing what you're doing, you'll keep getting what you're getting.

Your hard work and perseverance has gotten you where you are now, but to go higher you must be willing to leave your current level of comfort and venture into the unknown. You're never too old to grow. You're never too old to achieve your dreams. Sure, you'll have setbacks, but don't let them discourage you. A setback is just a set up for a comeback. Make up your mind, and stay determined to achieve your dreams no matter what. To do that, you can't get too comfortable with where you are.

The hardest part of turning any dream into a reality is taking the first step. Once you've taken the first step the other steps become easier. You'll find yourself getting closer, walking, and soon running toward your goal with strength and joy. You are what you've allowed yourself to become. No one can live your life but you. So what are you waiting for? Decide right now to take that next step.

Stop The Car

When you get tired while traveling on the road, what do you do? Pull over and get some rest so you can continue the trip safely. If you keep driving when you know you need to stop, there's a big chance you'll fall asleep at the wheel and get into an accident that could cost you your life. You need to know when to pull off the road of life and get some rest. If you feel tired and overwhelmed right now, take a break.

If you keep driving when you know your tank is on empty, eventually you'll run out of gas and get stuck on the road with no air conditioning in the heat. If you don't have everything checked out before you take that trip, you may break down. Then what are you going to do? Call for help, open your wallet, deal with the frustration, and pay for costly repairs because you didn't take the time to check things out before you hit the road. Your body is a lot like that car. Get a checkup if you haven't had one in a while. If you're feeling tired, irritable, and overworked, take a break from it all. Take a vacation. You'll feel so much better once you slow down, relax, and clear your mind.

Keep pushing yourself, keep going without sleep, keep stressing every day about bills, life, and business, and your body will short-circuit. You've got to take time to enjoy life, even if it's just spending an afternoon at the park relaxing under a tree. When you take a vacation, go somewhere you can relax. I don't mean visiting family— that's not a real vacation. Go to a place where you have no obligations. Your body can only take so much mentally, emotionally, and physically. Make time to enjoy the fruits of your labor. Stop pushing yourself for a while.

Don't Quit

Has a project or plan you've been working on come to a stop? Suddenly something has come up to prevent it, block it, or slow its progression? The deal is closed, the plans are set, then you get a call or e-mail saying there's a delay, the situation has changed, or they have decided to go another way or choose another option. When that happens, accept it, and move on or learn from it, and give it another try. Don't stop just because the winds have changed direction.

When moving to the next level of anything in life, you'll encounter stumbling blocks, setbacks, frustrations, and obstacles. That's a part of the growth process necessary to get you to your destination. Difficulties are there to help build strength and to sustain you once you achieve your goal. So don't complain about it, prepare for it. If something's too easy to accomplish the first time out, keep your eyes open and be leery, because it actually may be too good to be true. Whatever the difficulty is right now, you can and will get through it. Stick to your plan. Refuse to accept failure under any circumstances. Try again.

If your relationship is worth saving and your partner is in agreement, then work hard on it together with an open mind. You can and will get past the problems if you're both determined. None of us is perfect. All you can do is give life your best shot every day. Sometimes you'll stumble and fall. The key is to get up and keep running. Stop feeling sorry for yourself. You were born with the seeds of success, determination, willpower, and greatness. Don't give up. You've come too far. When you get to the point where you want to throw in the towel, that's when you're almost there.

Quit Complaining

Telling your business when you're down makes you feel worse. When things are going wrong, do you wear it all over? Is it obvious in your conversation, your appearance, your facial expression, and your attitude? Allowing it to consume you only makes matters worse. One of the steps to feeling better and drawing positive, happy energy your way is to quit complaining.

By focusing on the good and expecting the best, you set yourself up to receive it. Successful people are not in a hurry to help complainers. As a matter of fact, they avoid them. That's why your calls are never returned. They're looking at the caller ID, and they see your name. That's why they're not picking up. When you complain all the time, you bring positive people down with your outlook and attitude. They want no parts of it or you. Those who agree with you and keep you in that frame of mind are the very ones you need to step away from. Come out of the dark and focus on the light.

Here's what you should do right now and every time you feel that complaining spirit: Look at what you're complaining about as temporary and realize you have choices. Deal with it or change it. Whatever it is, complaining is only going to make you feel worse, so focus on the positives so you can get on to better thoughts and positive actions toward your destiny.

Tighten Up

It's time you take inventory of where you are in life. Are you on the fast track or are you on a treadmill going nowhere? When you get a cash windfall, do you keep it, invest it, or spend too much of it, finding yourself broke again, hoping for the next big payday? Are you waiting on your personal life to work itself out or are you doing what you have to in order to work it out? Spending time with negative people with bad habits? Why? You know better. You have two choices: continue living a loose life taking the slow road or take the fast track.

In order for something to grow, you have to care for it and feed it. Ignoring what's in front of you instead of dealing with it is like having your feet stuck in drying cement. The longer you stand there, the harder it'll be to get out. Stand there long enough and you'll be stuck forever. It's time you got tired of making the same mistakes.

Watch your finances. Know how much you can afford to spend without ending up with headaches and regrets. Stop trying to hang with the big boys, perpetrating a fraud on a train to the poorhouse. If you can't afford what you're getting, don't buy it until you can afford it. True freedom is being debt free. Go to sleep so you'll be rested the next morning. Organize your life. Follow a budget. Live within your means. Only loan what you can afford to give because you may not get it back. Save some money every time you get paid for the next rainy day, because a storm is on the way. Pay yourself first. As long as you live, you'll always owe someone somewhere. If you give everything you have, you'll never have anything for yourself.

Stop Waiting On Comfort

Do you really know why some things are difficult? It's because you perceive them as being that way. As a result, it becomes what you believe it is. Because a task is great doesn't mean it's difficult. It's just a bigger obstacle to overcome. It may take a little more time and effort to get through it, but it's not difficult because it's not bigger than you unless you make it so. If you change your attitude and perception about it, you can get through it just like you've gotten through everything else.

When you say something's difficult, you send a message to yourself and you begin to believe it. If you think it's hard, it will be hard because you made it so within yourself. The reality is, you really would rather not have to go through what you must go through to accomplish it. But if you decide to be positive, just jump into it, and start moving toward the finish line. Things will become easier and easier as you proceed. There is no comfortable time to begin something tough.

Think about how hard it would be to do what's in front of you now if it were a hundred years ago. Is it so hard now that you look at it that way? No. You have better resources. You have the ability. You have the skills and technology. The problem is, you're waiting on a time when it feels comfortable. The most rewarding accomplishments in life come through your persistence and determination to get them done no matter what the conditions or circumstances. You say you don't have the time? Make the time. You say you don't have what you need? Find the resources and use them. Not tomorrow. Do it today. Be thankful for this opportunity. Do it now.

Love and Relationships

"Love is passion, obsession, someone you can't live without. If you don't start with that, what are you going to end up with? Fall head over heels. I say find someone you can love like crazy and who'll love you the same way back. And how do you find him? Forget your head and listen to your heart. Run the risk, if you get hurt, you'll come back. Because the truth is there is no sense living your life without this. To make the journey and not fall deeply in love—well, you haven't lived a life at all. You have to try, because if you haven't tried, you haven't lived."

—[William Parrish] from the movie *Meet Joe Black* (1998)

I've been through many relationships in my lifetime, and I've loved hard, deep, passionately, and long. Some of those relationships were simply unforgettable, some were filled with lessons of how to love better, and some were just plain mistakes. I've been hurt and hurt others. I never set out to hurt anyone when it came to love, but relationships change, people's needs change, and things happen to cause us to drift apart sometimes. Like you, I thought with each love this one was the last. The best! The one for me!

Love is not always fair or comfortable, but when it is right ... wow! In spite of all of those loves, their conclusion, the experiences, and the memories both good and bad, I never gave up on love. The one thing God gave the world, love in the birth of His only begotten son, Jesus Christ, is my definition of true love. When you can give up something that means the most to you and your heart, you are truly in love! If God can love like that, who am I to give up on love because it sometimes fails? The beauty in it is worth giving it another try, a second chance.

Securing that beauty, that love as your own, no matter how short of a time you may have it or how long, is well worth the risk of pain. Through its heartaches, its beauty, bitterness, and joys, love has made me a better man. To live without it is not truly living. Never give up on love.

Let Go Of The Past

Bitterness and resentment block the flow of blessings in your life. Holding on to the hurts of your past poisons the present, your future, and your relationships, but when you let go of those emotional wounds, you open the door to a wonderful life. Let go of the past and its pain goes. No matter how much you bring it up in arguments or hold on to it for self-pity, move on. Holding on to hurt and pain has no positive effect on what's happening now or in your future. You're making yourself miserable. It blocks the pathways of love.

Holding on to painful events in your past influences your present actions and the way you respond to things. If you hold on to it, it'll paralyze you with fear and shame. We're all human. We all make mistakes. But when you choose to truly forgive those who have wronged you and release the pain, you can walk in freedom. Then you'll begin to really enjoy life and all it has to offer you. You'll trade your sorrow for joy. You'll trade your shame and hurt for peace and your bitterness for love.

If you say you forgive someone, do so. Really forgive them, and let it go. Your life is not defined by your past. It's gone. The pain is over. So stop reliving it. Stop forcing those you love to relive it with you. Stop bringing it up and throwing it in their face every time you get upset. They don't want to hear it, and you need to let it go. Only you can do it, so start now. Haven't you been miserable long enough? Let go of the pain and disappointments.

It's Not Easy

It's not easy to love people when they're not being nice. It's not easy just to overlook an insult. It's not easy to keep a good attitude and be patient when things aren't going your way. The natural reaction is to pay someone back, to get even when you've been done wrong; but ask yourself whether it's worth it. Will it end there? Sometimes it hurts to keep your cool, and sometimes it's uncomfortable. Every action has an equal and opposite reaction. Stop and think before you react. It's not easy, but you can do it if you try. Once you react on impulse without thought, you can't take it back. Just think of the many times you responded harshly to something you heard someone say, a lie told about you, being done wrong, or any injustice. You probably ended up later regretting what you've done. If you're hotheaded, you need to learn to keep your cool. The good seeds you sow today will bring a healthy harvest in the future.

Remember, the things you do always come back to you. Count to ten if you have to. Walk away if you have to. Decide today to begin handling unpleasant situations with patience and thought before you act. If you leap before you look and always end up bruised, it's time you changed the way you handle things. Thinking first, sometimes turning the other cheek, overlooking an insult, keeping a good attitude, and letting God handle it will be well worth the effort.

Stop Keeping Score

Are you the one in your relationship stuck in the past? When you get into an argument, do you bring up matters you've said have been forgiven? Do you forgive but not forget? Do you keep score of how many times you've been done wrong but fail to compare it to how many times you've wronged others? Do you think that really makes you feel better? Here's some real talk. No, it doesn't. It only makes you bitter. Cut that rope around your neck so you can breathe.

No one wants to be constantly reminded of their mistakes and shortcomings, especially if they're now trying to do the right thing and move beyond their mistakes. If they were sincere in their apology to you, they feel bad enough. If you keep this behavior up, you'll alienate and run them off. Bringing up the pains of the past has no positive effect on the future. Stop keeping score if you want to have any chance of keeping the people you care about around you, loving you unconditionally. Before you lose some of the most important people in your life, you'd better recognize what you're doing, and start living life forward and leave the past and its pains behind. It's history. Stop denying yourself complete peace of mind, joy, and happiness.

It Takes Two

Are you in a situation that has become bitter because you feel your needs aren't being met? Your partner is trying to understand you, but you're too busy fussing, fighting, and being mean to see it. Is someone dissatisfied with you because they feel they're doing all the giving and you're doing all the taking? Maybe you are, and maybe you aren't, but the fact remains: Love is work. Achieving success is work. Stop for a minute, and take inventory of yourself. Ask yourself, "Am I doing all I can do to please and bring harmony to this situation? Am I being selfish?" Take some time and put yourself in the other person's shoes. Try to see life through their eyes, and you may find that it wasn't just them. It's you as well. You're not giving as much as you're expecting.

Don't be so selfish, self-centered, and wrapped up in yourself to the point where you can't sense someone else's feelings. Step away from the situation, and take inventory of yourself. If you started giving the love or effort you wish to receive, you'll find yourself getting back what you're giving and more. If you want someone to listen, then you listen. If you want to be touched, give affection. If you want someone to be nice to you, be nice to them. If you want to be understood, then understand. You can't keep taking, not giving of yourself, and expect to be happy. Happiness in any relationship can't be created alone.

Say What's On Your Mind

Have you been walking around day to day with things on your mind you're afraid to express? Are you walking around with an attitude because you're upset? Get it out! I'm not a mind reader, your loved ones aren't mind readers, and your manager at work isn't a mind reader. Do you realize how much stress you're causing yourself and those around you by holding it in? Put a stop to this madness, and get it all out in the open.

Day after day, you're allowing this frustration to fester and grow like a mold. It's affecting your emotions, your joy, your body, your thoughts, your feelings, your life, and ultimately, your health. Life is too short to hold things in out of fear or frustration. If you're in a relationship where you can't be you and say what you feel, then you need to get out. Fast! Why stay in a situation where you have to hide your feelings?

Move On

Are you subconsciously letting someone bring you down? If you're not sure, ask yourself a few questions, and you'll have your answer. Is being in this relationship enriching my life? Does my partner motivate me and make me feel good about myself and my life? Is my being in this relationship giving me security? Am I not taking care of myself like I used to? Am I happy with this in my heart? If you've answered yes to these questions, you have your answer. If you've given it all you've got over and over again and nothing's changed, this is what you should do: Move on.

Leaving a situation that you've put a lot of time and effort into is hard. No one wants to start over again after investing years together, but look at the situation realistically. Is it worth putting the same amount of time in to keep this going when nothing changes? Answer that question, and you'll know what to do. Life does not stand still because you decide to. It moves on, and if you're in an abusive relationship, be it verbal, mental, or physical, it's definitely time to move on.

Relationships take work on both sides. And the give-and-take of that work is hard sometimes. Is leaving painful? Yes it is. Will the pain of leaving last? No. Like any other injury, it leaves scars, but eventually, they heal. If you're miserable right now with the one you're with, don't live like that anymore. There's a glorious life waiting for you to come back to it. Get back on the path God has set for you.

Meet The Need

Are you making a conscious effort each day to satisfy the important people in your life? Ask yourself how you can keep that person's emotional tank full. Find out what the people around you need, and do your best to help. You can't continue taking from someone emotionally, never giving back, and then expect your needs to be met. It doesn't happen that way. Never has and never will.

People express and receive love differently. We all have different kinds of needs and different ways to meet those needs. It's what makes us all unique. Take the time to find out what the ones you love need and how you can best meet those needs. This is true not only for marriage, but in every other relationship of your life. You'll grow closer to your children, have more meaningful and fulfilling friendships, and find that your life will take on a wonderful new dimension and purpose when you focus on caring for others instead of always thinking about yourself.

Don't Force It

When something fits, it feels good on you. You look good in it and you feel good about yourself because you know it suits you. People see you in it and compliment you on how nice you look. You'd never think of forcing yourself to wear something that you didn't feel made you look good. You know you can't fit your size nine frame in a size two outfit. No matter how much you like it, you have to leave it on the shelf if it doesn't fit. The same analogy applies to life. If you're in a situation that's not working and you've tried to do all you can to make it so to no avail, put it back on the shelf.

If you're in a relationship and that relationship doesn't feel good, if you're not getting along, if you're just not seeing eye to eye with your partner or employer, no matter how much you want it to be otherwise, you've got to realize and come to grips with the fact that that situation is a size two and you're a size nine.

If you force it, it won't feel good inside or out. It'll cause you pain and anguish. You resent being in a situation that damages your health or that makes you bitter and lose sight of who you really are. So get that mess out of the way, work it out, adjust if you can or let go, and move to the next chapter of life.

Be Careful Of How You Treat Love

How do you view love? As a weapon, as a tool, or a precious gift? Do you use love to make someone happy and secure or to manipulate. Through love, make him strong. Through love, make her feel appreciated. If you're capturing a person's heart on purpose with no intent of honoring and caring for it, that's wrong and selfish, and it'll come back to haunt you in equal measure. If things start going wrong for you, maybe it's because you played with someone's emotions and broke someone's heart somewhere in the past. Don't ask why. Know why. You used a precious gift for selfish gain.

Running a game on someone that you know has a big heart is an abuse of the gift of love. Man, if you don't really love her, let her go so she can find someone who does. Woman, you don't want him, you only want what he can do for you. That's wrong. Let him go. Too many good men and good women have been burnt by other men and women with bad intentions. Then, when a truly good person comes along, that person suffers for what you've done mistreating love. The heart is colder, the defense against hurt is in full effect, and the willingness to give love unconditionally in return is tarnished because you've been hurt and what you once gave freely from your heart has been abused. I know it's hard to open up again, but in order to find true happiness you've got to get past the pain, give it a chance, and love like it will never ever hurt you. That's the only way you'll ever find what you're looking for. Is there a chance you'll be hurt again? Yes. But there's also a chance you'll find the true happiness you've been dreaming about.

Stay Strong So You Can Move On

If you're in a relationship, it takes teamwork to sustain it. When times are good, you're happy; but how do you react when times aren't so good? Do you stand beside the one you love and work through it together, or do you make matters worse by doing less than you can to help get past it. Pointing the finger, yelling, and saying selfish, nasty things make matters worse. Don't let a bump in the road turn your world upside down. Difficulties will come. Expect them, but don't let them make you bitter. I'm not saying this as a license to do anything without thought and expect support. I'm talking about the unforeseen financial circumstances and life obstacles.

Work together, not against one another. If the two of you have decided to budget, and one of you keeps spending unnecessarily, that's a problem. It's bound to start an argument once an unexpected expense comes your way. So discipline yourself, stick to that budget, and stay the course. To grow, you have to learn to hold your tongue sometimes, even though it hurts. Try and be willing to learn new things; be supportive even though you may not understand it all; trust when you could have doubts; have faith in the one you love and in the One above. Bad times don't come to make you weak, they come to make you strong.

Try To Be There

There are times when people surrounding your life need your time, a listening ear, or your help. Are you so selfish that you can't be there for someone else in their time of need? Do you go to others for help but fail to make yourself available when they have a need? That's a self-centered, self-serving, ungrateful attitude, and you need to check yourself. If you call yourself a friend, then be a true friend.

Do you have any idea what happened in your child's life today? Did you stop to even ask? A child's world is a lot smaller than ours, and the little things you overlook and may have forgotten about childhood are as important to them as a major life issue is to you. Children's needs are simple in nature and pure at heart. Show them love by giving them time. Don't miss out on the precious growth years of your child's life, because you'll never get them back. Be there when they ask for your help and need your advice, so they can make the right life decisions.

If you love someone and they need to talk, make the time to hear them out with an open mind. If your spouse usually holds things inside but has finally gotten up the nerve to talk to you about something important, hold your peace, listen to her and not at her. Be there for a friend who was there for you. Don't dare turn your back. Remember how they were a blessing in your moment of distress. To be blessed, you must be a blessing.

Honor The One You Love

Marriage and relationships take work, understanding, and commitment. It is so important that you never forget that and do all you can to show your love. If you are committed to a life together, when you consistently feed your partner with love, it opens up important places in the heart. Women have needs and men have needs. You may not agree with and understand them all, and frankly, you shouldn't try to. Some things you'll never understand. Differences make us unique. You may not have the desire to do thoughtful things all the time, but you must understand that little gestures make a big difference.

Men, she needs attention. Take notice of the new dress, compliment her on that delicious meal, and acknowledge her efforts to make your life comfortable. Women and men were created differently on purpose. She's an emotional work of art, so wonderful, strong, brilliant, and unique, she has the ability to produce life. When she's upset, console her, talk to her, adore her, and be truthful, even if it hurts. Make this a habit, and you'll avoid the pain of deceit and refrain from lying. You won't have the desire to. Once you have her heart, once you've earned her trust, and if you continually, sincerely caress her mind, she'll be there for you in your times of need.

Women, stroke your man's ego. We know you're capable of handling things, but you have to allow your man to be the man. Show him respect. You can't expect respect of you don't give it. Never belittle him in private or public. If your man works hard, let him know how much you appreciate his providing for you and the family. Never lose your sense of womanhood. You know how to melt his heart. If you use what you've got, you'll get what you want. If you give him everything he needs at home, he'll have no reason to stray. Never deny each other pleasure. Remember your vows, whether it was to be committed to your relationship or until death do you part.

Realize It's Over

When you've done all you can do, when you've tried in every way to work it out, with no success, it's time to get real. If you've tried counseling, prayer, therapy, intervention, and going against what you feel inside just to keep hope alive and things still aren't right, that's when you must face the pain and end the relationship.

You can't force a situation to be what you want it to be. It's like a puzzle. Only the pieces made to fit it will. Sometimes we go after what we were never meant to have, ignoring all the signs along the way. Your true happiness may be right under your nose, but you're just too caught up in your present situation to see it. You're trying so hard to make that dead-end relationship work. You've been on this treadmill going nowhere long enough. It's time to deal with the pain of moving on.

You love her and she can't see it. You love him, and he won't accept it. Stop doing this to yourself, because there's someone out there who will love you for who you are if you let them; but before a new relationship blooms, the healing from the broken one must begin.

Try A Little Kindness

If things aren't working in your life—your love life, your business, or your relationship—maybe it's because you're mean and selfish. Maybe you've been told so, but you won't accept it. How could
you be the problem? How could things be going wrong because of
you? Impossible you say? No, it's very possible. Maybe it's the way
you respond to, talk to, and treat people. Maybe it's your tone of
voice. Being, harsh, cold, and mean will get you nowhere. Try being
kind if you really want to change things. Try kindness instead of
yelling at your children, your wife, or your co-workers, instead of being the scrooge in everyone's life, instead of being mad at the world
because it doesn't cater to your every need.

Want love and consideration? Then give love and consideration.
Want to be listened to when you're speaking from the heart? Then
listen when someone's speaking to you from their heart. Not speaking to one another? Want to feel wanted? Then make those around
you feel wanted. If any of this applies to you, then change the way
you treat people and a whole new world of happiness and blessings
will open up to you.

Honor Your Wife

If you are blessed to find and take a wife, then honor her. If you make a vow before God to love, honor, and cherish 'til death do you part, don't play with that promise to God. You may find it okay to lie to anyone here on earth but not to God. If you can't keep the promises, then don't go to the altar. You both have to want this with all that is within you. If you don't feel that way, then please don't do it!

Think hard before you get married, and when you do, give her the love the sun gives a flower, the patience when she needs it, a smile and comfort, and water her emotions when she sometimes loses her way. Respect and honor her as she respects and honors you.

It took love to get her, and it will take more of that same love and understanding to keep her as her emotions mature, twist, turn, and evolve along the road of life. Like you, she has a lot to deal with. If you have children, add being a good mother to the list. If she has a career, add being successful to the list. If she has your back financially, is supportive, and really tries to please you in every way, add being a wonderful woman to the list. The next time you look at her deeply, remember what took your heart, and feed that hunger for more of the same. If you love her the way she needs to be loved, a good woman will do almost anything you ask to keep you happy.

Get It Out, Stop Holding It In

Got something on your mind that's tearing you up inside? Can't sleep at night? Gaining or losing weight for no reason? Are you feeling irritable and angry? The reason you may be going through these things is because you're not facing what's bothering you. Holding things in that you need to get out can kill you mentally, physically, and spiritually. Inner stress can disrupt everything in your life if you allow it to continue. Why take yourself through this?

If you have something to say, say it. If you're in a relationship or situation where you can't calmly speak your mind, you need to re-evaluate it. If you're living to please someone else and getting no pleasure out of the situation, then you need to pack up and get to stepping. Granted, you should talk about it first, but if you've done that over and over with no results, start working on your exit strategy. This kind of life is not healthy for you or anyone around you. So before it gets to the point of chaos, talk about it.

Once you do, you'll feel a lot better inside. Maybe not at first, but you will in time as you move on to a life free of the stresses you're going through now. You then will be able to rediscover who you really are and what you really enjoy. Once you get back to you, you'll look back on all of this and wonder why you ever put yourself through it. Stop wasting away precious moments of life in strife. Find a wonderful, happy life.

Just Be Yourself

If you're single and searching for someone special or just living life without any expectations and are okay with it, I know you've had your share of disappointments. Not all of us have a wife, husband, or companion. Being single allows you to control your world free of compromise, but it can really be lonely at times. Then there are the disappointments that come from the relationships you hope and wish could have. Maybe you're trying too hard to be what someone else wants.

Falling in true love takes time. It takes time to learn to appreciate one another's needs, wants, likes, and dislikes. What makes him or her happy or sad? It takes time to get to know someone new and more time to find out if who you met is who they really are. If a new friend says they don't want a relationship, respect that and decide if that road is for you. Don't try to transform someone into what you want them to be. Allow that change to happen naturally. Don't be in a rush to find love. It will find you if you if you allow yourself to be found.

If you're healing from hurt or disappointment, you're vulnerable and fragile. Don't try to make any fast decisions while rediscovering yourself. Give the healing process some time. More and more people today say they are satisfied with being alone, but in reality, no one really wants to be alone. Be careful not to become sheltered and secluded. It's hard to find someone who's hiding because of the pains of the past. Don't be afraid of love. Just do the things that make you happy. Yes, you could get hurt along the way, but you could also find true happiness. Somewhere along the way, you'll run into love.

Give The Gift Of Time

On special occasions and even day to day, when you think of giving a gift, the choices are limitless in terms of material things. As long as you live, you'll never run out of things you can buy or do to make someone happy and show your affection. As life happens, you'll go to great lengths financially to make someone you love feel special. Give a gift that will not leave you in debt or stress you out in preparation—a gift of your time that will be cherished long after the glitter of material things fade.

If it seems no matter what you provide, what you take care of, or what you buy, the person on the receiving end never seems satisfied, maybe it's because that's not what they really want from you. If buying your way to happiness fails to get you the appreciation you truly feel you deserve, maybe material giving isn't the solution to bringing true joy to the one you love. If you're constantly on the go and you feel using gifts to fill the emotional gaps gets you around the bases, but never to home plate, try giving your time instead.

Time can't be replaced or exchanged. You can't charge it or write a check for it. The beauty of giving of yourself is it costs you nothing, but its returns are priceless. It shows the depth of your love like nothing else. So if you've been told by the ones you love you're not giving enough of this precious gift, then commit from this day forth to make space in your life to be there for them.

A New Beginning

In order to make room for the new, you have to rid yourself of the old. You can't put more water in a full bucket. You have to empty some out first. To make room for blessings, you must rid yourself of the things taking up space in your life. It may not be easy. It may hurt to do it. You're holding on to what feels good to you, but you know it isn't good for you. You want it, so it's staying in the way of your moving forward in life. Not everything you want is what you need to fulfill your destiny. Right now, make a decision to deal with and get rid of those things.

If your home life's a mess and you're making matters worse by having an affair, you're ignoring the problems, making more, and overlooking the issues that need to be addressed in exchange for momentary pleasure. If you put as much effort into dealing with the problems in your relationship as you do into pleasing an outside man or woman, maybe things would improve at home. Stop pretending the problems don't exist. Stop running away from them. Deal with it! If the one you're with truly loves you but isn't the one you love, then set them free to find someone who will love them faithfully, heart and soul. Stop allowing them to live your lie. Maybe your circumstance isn't a relationship. It could be business. Whatever it is, it's time to be up front about your feelings.

Once you free your mind and your life of clutter, the wrongdoing, the secrets and the lies, you'll find yourself truly enjoying life more in the light of happiness and peace. So don't be afraid of moving on. Open that new chapter of life. Do these things and watch the blessings flow toward you.

Show Your Love

Everyone at one time or another falls short in expressing love. There are some unique cases where two people continuously show how much they love each other and seldom fall short. If you're in that minority, consider yourself blessed. It's not that way for everyone. The pressures of life, the disagreements, unexpected occurrences, hustle and bustle, and disappointments in life take a toll. Time also has a way of making you comfortable. Before you were blessed with the one you love, you tried everything in your power to win his or her heart. Now you're used to one another. This is where the trouble begins. Never get used to the one you love.

Showing your love doesn't have to be a costly proposition all the time, although going all out and being extravagant every once in a while is nice. It's not the big things you do that carry the most weight. It's the little thoughtful things, the smiles and laughter you share each day. Saying "I love you" with a kiss each morning, listening while your partner's heart speaks, calling a loved one for no other reason than to say you care, telling them how much they're missed, or just catching up on what's been happening in their world.

A hug, an unexpected surprise, a late night walk along the beach, or a stroll in the park speaks volumes. Pay attention enough to know when something's wrong or knowing what that something is without being told. That's when you're truly in love: when you know what your loved one is feeling without asking. Expressing the feelings of your heart isn't hard. If you're the receiver of love and never the giver, your relationship is headed for certain disaster. Don't let that happen. Love is a two-way street. The traffic must flow both ways. Life is too short to live without the passion you desire. There's one thing you should never forget as long as you live: to get what you want, you have to give it back.

Silence Is Agreement

Is there something going on in your life or home that's irritating you? Is there something going on around you that you've chosen to ignore and continue to allow to happen? If it bothers you, say something about it. By allowing whatever it is to continue without a word, you're condoning it. If you've said something about it and it continues, saying nothing is like giving it the okay. If there's crime in your neighborhood and you know who is committing it, you should say something or take collective action to stop it. Don't just live in fear because you think there's nothing you can do. There *is* something you can do. Speak up, report it to the authorities, form a neighborhood watch, but do something. By being silent, you're enabling the activity. Maybe you're silent because you're afraid or because you feel saying something will only make matters worse. How will you know unless you say something? Look at it this way, if you fail to say or do anything, whatever is troubling your world will continue to bring a dark cloud into each day of your life. So weigh your options, take a chance, make your feelings known. You could gain the peace and comfort you so richly deserve if you break your silence.

It's Time To Let It Go

Allow me to bring an important issue to light: your happiness. You only go down life's road once. Only you have the ability to make this journey a good one. It's never too late to start living a happy life. If you're in a lifeless relationship right now after putting all you have into it, then you need to stop fooling yourself into believing things are going to get better on their own. Are you the one always trying to work things out and your partner is always bringing problems and drama? Face the facts. How many more days, weeks, months, or years are you going to allow this mistake to continue?

If you're married, you will go through changes together. Expect them. You made a vow to stick it out through thick and thin, so your situation has a different level of commitment. If you're not married or if you're living with someone, you have a door to get out and move on if all else fails and things are beyond repair. It's time to let go if you're arguing over little things all the time; if your emotional or physical needs are no longer being met; if you're always wrong and your partner's always right; if you're disrespecting each other; if you're seeing someone else on the side for comfort; if you find yourself still with this person only for the material things; if you're no longer doing all the wonderful things you did when love was new and you have no desire to; if you're carrying the load alone.

You've grown apart and you know it. If the thrill is gone, stop prolonging the pain. Don't get me wrong. Give it all you've got and try to work things out before saying goodbye. Breaking up is hard emotionally and sometimes financially, but it's better to cut your losses now so you can begin the healing process. Stop investing any more of your precious life in a relationship that's going nowhere. It's like a car that's beyond repair. It may still look good on the outside, but it's not worth it to get it fixed. It's time to get one you can depend on.

Stop Hurting Yourself

If you are married but unhappy due to abuse, being married doesn't mean you can't leave someone who's hurting you. The institution of marriage is one of respect, not abuse. When you took those vows and made that commitment, you became two individual souls united as one. As a result, you should treat your spouse as you wish to be treated. Abusing the one you say you love is wrong and has no place in a marriage. This applies to men and women. When you abuse your spouse you're abusing the love you pledged and the spiritual promises you made for life.

If you're being physically, mentally, or verbally abused, and you believe it will stop but it reoccurs, stop fooling yourself. Stop believing the empty promises. Seek help. Stop making excuses for the pain. If you're the one causing the pain, why did you lie when you made the promise to love, honor, and cherish until death do you part? You need help. If you're cruel to, constantly hitting, or yelling at your spouse, you need help. If you're being abused, you need help. The both of you should get help, and if that doesn't work, then get out. Maybe you married a stranger. A marriage license doesn't require you to endure pain. The situation you're in is extremely dangerous. Don't accept pain. You've got to get past the fear. Get help or get out.

Whether you're the husband or the wife, no matter what you're going through or what's occurring in your life, it doesn't give you the right to abuse the person who loves you. If you have children, you're hurting them too. You're scarring them for life by allowing them to be exposed to the abuse you're receiving. Do you want them to grow up thinking this is the way relationships should be? Of course you don't. After you've tried counseling, intervention, and prayer, and you still continue to suffer the pain of abuse at the hands of the one who says he or she loves you, get a divorce. Move on with life. Leave! There's someone out there who really wants to love you.

Stay Out Of It

Sound advice can only be given if you know both sides of the story. One of the best ways to ruin a friendship or destroy a relationship with someone is to give bad advice. There are two sides to every story, and you need to hear all sides of an issue. If you agree with only the person asking your opinion, you risk feeding their feeling of being right all of the time. You have a responsibility to be honest and accurate if the person asking trusts and respects your opinion.

If you're not married and have never been married, stop telling married people how to solve their problems. What makes you an expert on solving marriage problems? If you're not in a relationship, you have no woman in your life or you can't keep a man, stop giving advice to someone who is in a relationship. What gives you the right? Likewise, if you're in a relationship and seeking counsel from someone who has no one and can't keep a mate, their opinion may exacerbate your situation. Sometimes you do get sound advice from a friend. But think about it. Would you go to a dentist to get your suit altered or a mechanic to represent you in court? If your situation doesn't lend relevance to the advice given, ignore it.

Bottom line, if it's not your business, if it does not involve you directly, if you can't relate to the situation from experience, if it's only hearsay or gossip, if you can't provide solid solutions instead of vague ideas, then instead of possibly doing more harm than good, maybe it's best you just pray for them and stay out of it.

Tell Those You Love You Love Them Every Day

Life is an ambiguous, mysterious gift. Despite the uncertainty, never neglect those close to you. When they're gone and, God forbid, if they are taken away suddenly, you'll find yourself grieving over missed opportunities to spend time with them. Only then will it be too late because they're gone. Tell them now that you love them. A couple I know lost their twenty-four-year-old son. He was eating a sandwich and started choking. The father got out most of the meat as they rushed him to the hospital, but they didn't realize one piece was lodged in his throat. As a result, there was no oxygen to his brain for thirty minutes. He was on a ventilator in a hospital that night until the following Saturday evening, where he was taken off and died. He left behind a twenty-month-old daughter and a four-month-old son. I'm not sure how much love his family members showed him or how often they said they loved him. Life is never to be taken for granted.

Showing love every day provides you with joy and leaves you with no regrets. If you're harboring resentment, anger, bitterness, jealousy, grudges, or ill feelings toward loved ones, let it go and work it out with them now. Get past it while you still have them in your life. Situations come and go. None of us are perfect. Life is a one-shot deal. There is no second chance at it once it's gone—no encore, no reruns. You have one chance at living it in a spirit of love and compassion.

Strive To Live In Harmony

Life gives you bright moments and lasting personal peace when you strive for balance: physical balance, balance in your thoughts, actions, finances, business, and relationships. It requires discipline, sacrifice, and compromise. You can pour fresh water into a full glass until you either drink some of it our pour some out. The longer you let it sit open and unattended, the more contaminated it gets. Some of it you see and some of it you don't. Empty your glass each day so fresh water can be added.

Harmony doesn't mean you have to agree with everything. Sometimes you have to agree to disagree and accept the fact that there's a difference of opinion and move on. Pushing issues can often cause problems and disrupt the balance in your life. If you're committed to a situation, harmony doesn't mean you have to be the same, think the same, act the same, or do the same things. It means you must learn to accept and adjust to the small differences together with the understanding that no matter what, you're determined to stay committed to the cause.

Stop shutting things down in your life by insisting on having your way all the time. Don't be too pushy! I hate it, and I know you do too. Harmony is not achieved by force, intimidation, control, weakness, or through selfishness. Harmony is achieved though compromise, acceptance, listening, understanding, giving, caring, patience, respect, and compassion. Understand that we are all different, and respect the beauty in those differences.

Don't Fret It If They Don't Get It

Ever find yourself dealing with someone who seldom sees things your way? Someone who has an ever-changing attitude of opposition to your thoughts, actions, or ideas? They always insist you are the one who has the problem when, in fact, they are the problem and they refuse to see it any other way. Why? Because they want things their way. For days, weeks, months, maybe years, you've been going through frequent disagreements and arguments about the same things. You've agreed to disagree. It's time you stop dealing with it and move on.

Trying to convince someone to see things your way can drain the life out of you. If you've got long-standing irritating differences between you and someone else, it's time you stop and look at the situation for what it is. Is it worth it to continue down this road to nowhere? Will it ever come to an end? If it's stressing you out, if you're unhappy about it, tired of it, if it's affecting the rest of your life, let it go, or let them go. It's interfering with your destiny. Stop the car and get that broken glass off the road you're traveling.

Stop letting them tap into your stuff. If life was going fine before they came along, no matter how kind they may be, leave them and their stubborn attitude, crazy ideas, inability to compromise, the arguments, one-sided thinking, and negativity. If you must, endure until time cures it. If they can't see what you're seeing, stop trying to convince them otherwise.

Agree To Disagree And Let It Be

We're all different in one way or another. It's a rare occasion when you find someone who is compatible with you in every way. The chances of finding happiness are slim if you're looking and waiting for the perfect person. We all have something we don't agree on or like at some point in our relationships. You can let those differences become a problem, constant battle, feud, or argument, or you can do the wise thing: not wear yourself out about it.

Stop arguing and fighting. If you don't agree, then accept that no one is right—or wrong. See the impasse as a difference of opinion, not a threat, not a win-lose situation. Most importantly, if and when you agree to disagree, stop bringing it up. That only causes more unrest. If the issue at hand presents a deeper problem for you that you feel you can't live with, then maybe that situation you're in is not the one for you. If you leave some things be, they have a way of working themselves out on their own. Whatever your differences, face it, you'll never have your way all the time. Sometimes, to maintain harmony you have to keep the battle inside, deal with it on your own within, and let the Man above handle it.

"A sacrifice to be real must cost, must hurt,

and must empty ourselves. Give yourself fully to God.

He will use you to accomplish great things

on the condition that you believe much more

in His love than in your weakness."

— Mother Teresa

Spirituality

I asked my pastor, John K. Jenkins Sr. of the First Baptist Church of Glenarden, to share some wisdom on spirituality. He chose some words from one of his sermons that lifted me. Everything he says in his sermons hits home with me because I know it's not him speaking to me. He is only the vessel, the conduit. It is the word of God through his sermons that causes my heart to ache with happiness and my eyes to tear with joy.

Everyone has something they worship or believe in. It is not my intention to push God upon anyone. I choose to live my life according to my beliefs and hopefully my light will shine brightly enough so that you will want to have some of what you see in me. Everyone needs someone to believe in. Once you embrace that belief, miraculous things will happen in your life. You will doubt no more, and doors which were once closed will open wide.

Declare Your Independence

Before you go to sleep tonight, decide within yourself once and for all that enough is enough. Tomorrow will be your day of change. No matter what you may be facing, no matter what is trying to hold you back, let it be your day of independence, liberation, and freedom. Declare your independence from sickness, be it physical or mental. Declare your independence from that abusive relationship. Declare your independence from poverty. Declare your independence from loneliness. Declare your independence from fear. Declare your independence from lack. Then, declare your total dependence on God.

Release your past and all the negative memories, people, and thoughts associated with it and start living in the beauty of life again. Forgive those you've been holding a grudge against and accept forgiveness from those who have forgiven you. Stop beating yourself up. Declare your independence from the scars of the past and move forward into a new light, a new life. It's time to live your dreams, so declare your independence from anything other than enjoying live. Life is too short to live within the negative and dark things that you have the ability to change. No one can do your work for you. No one can change you but you. The time is now and now is the time. Declare your independence and let today be the last day of living less than the best.

It's Not All About You

Is love your greatest aim? When you wake up in the morning, do you seek opportunities to show love and help others? Or do you only look for ways that you can get ahead, prosper, gain status or position? Remember, somewhere along the way someone helped you get where you are today. To gain favor and ensure continued good fortune, you've got to set your needs aside from time to time and pay the favor forward.

When you make love your greatest aim and seek to serve other people regardless of a tangible benefit, you close the door to the enemy's plan for your life and open the door for abundant blessings. In order for that to happen with any consistency, you have to help others. Life is not designed to revolve around just your desires. Those around you have needs too.

Choose to walk in love and peace. Refuse to be jealous or selfish, and at all costs, avoid strife and drama. Meditate on 1 Corinthians 13. As you allow this new way of thinking to shape your actions and develop your lifestyle of love, with a little servitude you will discover the champion in you. It's not all about your personal gain at all costs all the time. That's selfish. Although it may not stop your success, it'll slow you down in life and may divert you from your destiny. Don't be so stuck on yourself.

You've Done All You Can Do

Stop letting your wants run your life. The Word say's God will supply your needs. The book doesn't say he'll supply your wants. That's where we all, me included, make or have made our mistakes in life. I've made many in that respect. You'll never be any good for someone else until you straighten out yourself. The person you've been trying to help may be beyond your help.

Sometimes situations are such that you have to turn to professionals and counseling to address mental and personal issues and scars. Sometimes it's more than what you alone can fix. There's nothing you can do no matter how many times you've tried. There are only so many people you or I have the ability to help along the road of life. You have to realize that "it is what it is." Let go.

We are our biggest enemy and hindrance from getting what God offers us. If the way you do things has gotten you nowhere, then wake up and realize it's not working and take a different path. It's not fair to expect people to help you all the time. You need to learn to survive on your own, because in life you will come upon times over and over when this is what you must do alone. You'll have no choice. If you support this destructive behavior in someone's life, you're doing more damage than good. It may be time for the tough love.

Encourage Yourself

Wouldn't it be great to have someone providing you with a constant supply of encouragement? If you get in the habit of encouraging yourself each day, that's exactly what you can have. Pat yourself on the back each time you complete a task. All day long, you think and say things to yourself. You have the power to choose what those thoughts and those words will be.

Choose to make your thoughts and words positive, uplifting, and encouraging. And make good use of the many opportunities you have each day to provide yourself with support and direction. When you're beating up on yourself, decide then and there to stop. How's that helping the situation? It's not. Maybe you don't get the encouragement your heart longs for from others, at home or at work. So what? Give yourself a few words of real, sincere encouragement.

Instead of talking about someone who's falling short, get in the habit of offering encouragement to those you come in contact with whenever you get the chance. What goes around comes around. That'll make them more likely to send encouragement your way. In order to receive a blessing, you've got to be a blessing. Encourage yourself on those days and in those moments when you're feeling less than your best.

Go With The Flow

Life is a beautiful journey, a one-shot deal. It can be a wonderful experience if you just go with the flow. Stop worrying about everything and over-analyzing those wonderful, unexpected moments before you make a decision. Sometimes God gives us an occasional treat in the midst of the obstacles in life. If it feels good and it won't hurt anyone, just do it.

If you follow your instincts and become close friends with them, you'll seldom go wrong because it comes from the real you. If you take too many opinions and perspectives into account, you'll start to second guess yourself and what you set out to do. If it's your passion and on the path toward your goal, stop asking so many people what they would do and follow your gut instincts. It's your life, your happiness, your dreams, and goals.

It's wise to sometimes think things through and consider the advice of others. Just don't let it dilute the passion you feel about the moment. If you worry too much about making the right decision, you may end up not making any decision or making that decision too late. Trying to avoid a mistake could be your biggest mistake. You may end up letting a good opportunity pass you by.

Watch What You Say

Do you realize how much power your words have? They're one of the windows to your soul. Look closely at the life of someone who curses a lot in a conversation. What's the purpose? Does it make you shine, make you cool, show you're tough? No, it doesn't. It taints any good first impression you're trying to make. Your words have power. Are you using them as a destructive force or as an instrument of blessing, peace, and motivation?

No one loves a foul mouth. I hate it and to be honest, like most good people, I can't wait to be out of your presence. If you keep speaking negative words over your life or in your life, eventually defeat will be the result. In the same way, if you speak pleasant words of faith and victory, you will see a harvest of blessing not only in your own life, but also in the lives of those around you. How many times do you curse in a conversation? Try having one without cursing. If it's hard to do, you've got problems. Your words could be holding you back.

I challenge you from this day forward to watch the words you speak. When you find yourself in a difficult situation, don't say the first thing that pops into your head. It's been a habit for a while now, so this change won't happen overnight. If you clean up your mouth, you'll make new friends, keep the ones you have, and move forward past the doors your words have kept locked. When you use positive words, you'll overcome every challenge that you face, and you'll live the abundant life that God has in store for you. Control your words.

Cherish Today

I lost a good friend a few years ago. He wasn't someone who I saw frequently, but we always remained close. When I got to work one evening, I found out he had died in his sleep and it caused me to reflect on this thing we call life, this life we take for granted every single day. I always say tomorrow is not promised to you, it's a promise hoped for. But we selfishly assume it's going to come. We take life for granted, so we waste most of the goodness and blessings provided for us and around us today. Yesterday, he was here, alive and vibrant, and today he's gone. Just like that, God called him home. Take advantage of everything good and wonderful at your disposal right now.

If you've ever lost someone close to you, you know the feeling. That's the time when you really look at your life, what it means, and where it's going. It's time to make positive changes and realize just how truly short life really is. The beauty of what you come to realize when you experience a loss is that if you're lucky you're being given a chance each day you awake to another sunrise to live life to the fullest and love with all your heart. If you feel what I'm saying to you, join me in making a vow: Call the ones you love more often just to let them know you care. Spend more time with family. Let go of anger and resentment. Take time out for yourself. Kiss and hug your wife, husband, or significant other at every opportunity. Say what's in your heart and don't hold back. Even the next minute's not promised to you. The only thing that is certain in life is now. Don't count on tomorrow to get your life together. Don't wait on tomorrow to make a change. All you truly have is here and now.

Don't Waste Your Time

Don't waste your time worrying if something will go wrong; just start on whatever it is and take it one step at a time. That's the only way to get through it and finish. Worrying about how something will turn out before it happens sets you up for failure. It keeps you from giving your absolute best because you're afraid. Failure comes from not trying. Ignore that feeling of worry.

When it comes to helping those who refuse your help, leave it to God. If you take your hand off of it and get out of the way, he'll fix it His way. Sometimes when you're trying too hard to help, you make matters worse. Sometimes you have to just get out of the way and let what happens happen. Stop traveling a road that's leading nowhere.

You're forcing it when you impose your desires on someone else who is resisting. You may get what you want, but is it real and lasting if you forced it to happen? Why would you want something forced instead of given freely? You'll find down the line they're tired of being your creation.

Problems Have a Purpose

No matter where your faith lies, or if you have any faith at all, when tough times come, take the time to examine what got you there. In the midst of your trouble, examine what caused you to be where you are. Most of the time, those troubles are because of your choices.

Why are you in legal trouble? How'd you get into so much debt? Why aren't you where you should be in life? It's because of your choices. None of us can predict the future. All we can do is decide today and live with whatever decisions are made. Life is a series of successes and failures. With each failed attempt, you learn something to make you stronger and wiser. If you examine yourself closely each time you face difficulties, you find what you need to prevent it from happening again.

Don't beat yourself up. Do what you must to get past the trouble. Maybe after this is over, you'll examine your next decisions more closely before you make them. Separate your wants from your needs. Stop doing what you did to get into this predicament. Next time, think harder before you sign on the dotted line. Next time, think about the potential effects of what you're about to say before you say it. Next time, stay where you are instead of going where you shouldn't. Difficult times make you stronger. Pick yourself up and examine the inner you.

Stop Blocking Your Blessings

In life, as long as you think something is standing in your way you won't be able to travel that road. The only thing that's really in your way is your thinking. If you move forward past your fears in any situation, you'll find with each step you're getting closer to your goal. Major obstacles get smaller. When you believe something's going to be hard or difficult, it will be. So change your perception of the outcome.

If you're mean and curse people out in anger, you're blocking your blessings. If you often lie or dodge responsibility for your actions, you're blocking your blessings. Every time you intentionally hurt or disappoint someone, you're putting in an order for hurt and disappointment to come your way. Neglecting those around you who love and need you and being selfish and materialistic are all blessing blockers. It's really not hard to put yourself in a posture to receive the best in life.

The days of your life will be much better if you treat people the way you want to be treated. Be a giver instead of a taker and much will be given to you because of your unselfish kindness. This may be hard for some of you to grasp because you've been doing it your way so long. You're angry with the road life is taking you because of your actions. If you try living life differently with the right intentions, your world will eventually transform into something wonderful.

Do It Afraid

There's something happening in your life right now that you're apprehensive about or afraid to challenge. If it's not happening now, eventually it will. When obstacles or difficulties present themselves, we often times tend not to deal with them right away. As a matter of fact, there's something in your life right now that you have decided not to deal with. Deal with it because it's not going away. The unknown and difficult often travels with a degree of fear. FEAR is False Evidence Appearing Real.

Where is your faith? Is it that weak? Have you forgotten that you can do all things through He who strengthens you? You can accomplish anything if you just put your mind to it and do it. If firemen were afraid of fires, everything burning would burn to the ground and lives could be lost. If the police were afraid of criminals, none of us would be safe and the world would be in chaos. It's because they have no fear in the face of fear that fear itself is defeated.

If you need to address a situation in your life, but you haven't out of fear of the outcome, then not dealing with it is keeping you uneasy and miserable. Is this the way you want to live? No, it's not! It's like going to the doctor. You hate needles, but once you take the shot, the infection goes away and you feel much better. Don't let the disease of FEAR control and stagnate you. Stop losing sleep over it. Do what you have to do. Get past it. Have faith that He who made you will never fail you.

Those Who Mind Don't Matter,
And Those Who Matter Don't Mind

As you walk and live this spiritual journey toward God, you will encounter a lot of things that will open your eyes to realities. Some will be good and some bad. When you give your life to Christ there are no sudden transformations from mortality to immortality. There is a gradual transition to grace. You'll make mistakes, struggle to break habits, change your circle of friends, be criticized, face ridicule, and become the subject of scrutiny. Many will eagerly point out the things that you haven't gotten in line with the Scriptures. Don't let it trouble you. Let it not be a source of discomfort in your walk.

If the people, friends, and family surrounding you are constantly trying to pull you back from your newfound faith and new life, step away from them. Live your life as you know it should now be lived through the Word. Will they stop trying to convince you to come back to their way of living, drag you back to the old bad habits, the wrong places, the wrong people, and entice you to do the wrong things? Finding salvation will not stop those things from happening, but know that each time you resist the temptation to go back to that life you've been delivered from, that which brought you to the need to say enough is enough, you're taking one more step toward the day that the very thought of those things no longer has power over you. There is a family of believers surrounding you who are going through, or have been through, the same trials. Turn to that family of believers to lift you when you fall.

Meet Someone's Need

If you want to keep blessings and good things coming your way, then meet someone's need. If you want good things to come your way, then do good things for those you come in contact with. In order to keep good things coming your way, you must do good things for others from your heart—not because you want something in return, but because it's the right thing to do. It's like a natural high once you get in the habit of it.

When you are blessed with wealth and good fortune, much is required of you in return. You should be a blessing to someone else in their time of need. There is someone right now who genuinely needs your help, and you're able to help them, but you won't. Being selfish backfires. You wind up hurting yourself and losing things important to you. Maybe it's happening because you failed to use a portion of your good fortune or time to help those in need. Maybe it's an issue you have problems with. If you want your needs met, fulfill someone else's. It doesn't have to be in money, it can be with your time.

Volunteer your services and expertise to a nonprofit organization. Pay someone's light or gas bill. Buy groceries for someone who's having a hard time. Take a friend whose spirit is down out to dinner. Visit someone sick or elderly who never gets a visit. Listen when someone needs you to hear them in a trying time. Help fulfill the dreams of friends, family, neighbors, and co-workers. You must give to get.

"Nobody can go back and start a new beginning,

but anyone can start today and make a new ending."

— Maria Robinson

You

The first time I was given a major responsibility as president of my high school class; the first time I held a position of power as music director of a radio station; the first band I played in or managed; the first TV show I hosted and produced; the first day I was on the air in a major radio market; the beginning of my marriage; the birth of my child; the first time I made love; the first time I saw an island sunset; when I lost my mother and grandparents and friends. Ahh ... the good times, sad times, glad, and bad times. Many things you have experienced have been the building blocks of who you are. Foundations sometimes develop cracks that need sealing. As you truly grow, you should strive to get to a point where the failing happens less and the standing more. This chapter is about you, your foundation and keeping it strong. Stand through the wind, rain, heat, cold, sunshine, and storms.

Take A Stand, Walk Away

Are you ever tempted to do something you know is wrong? Maybe you're about to do something wrong right now. Do you find yourself around people or circumstances that tempt you to compromise? Your mind's telling you "no," but your body is saying "yes." Resist the urge to do something you'll live to regret once the thrill is gone.

You keep saying you'll kick that habit, but you keep putting yourself in temptation's way. You have the power within yourself to do what many mature, strong, sound men and women do when they're faced with temptation that's too great to deal with—run. That's right: run. You are a person of excellence and integrity, so don't feel bad about advancing to the rear. When temptation comes, your response needs to be the same—run.

Get away from people who are pulling you down. Stay away from those people and places you know you should avoid. Turn off television shows you know you shouldn't watch. Block the Internet sites. Refuse to compromise. When you do these things repeatedly, you'll form a new habit. Blessings and favor will fall on you and your family, and you'll prosper in whatever you do. The next time temptation comes your way, the next time you're invited to enjoy a weakness you're trying to get away from, don't think about it, don't even talk about it. Walk away.

Encourage Others Each Day

Life doesn't always deal you good cards. Each day, you have op-portunities to reach out and encourage someone else, either in per-son, by pen, text, or e-mail. Even in the grocery store, believe it or not, you can encourage someone. Smile and be friendly, strike up a conversation with someone else in line. Not only will the time in line pass much faster, but you'll also make a big difference in the life of the person you encouraged while waiting.

In order to receive blessings you have to be a blessing. That's how it works. At the office, on the street, in the restaurant, the de-partment store, anywhere you run into someone who may need some inspiration. Just think—that may be the only word of encourage-ment they receive all day. Remember you've been placed there for a reason. Instead of walking by someone without speaking, which we often do, say hello with a smile. If you run into someone who's losing their confidence, lift them up as much as you can to set them back on track.

That encouraging word may be just what they needed at that moment. Be flexible and learn to go with the flow. Loosen up. Don't be so cold and wrapped up in yourself. When you help those around you, you'll begin to see more peace, joy, and victory in your life.

Be Thankful

Your words have the power to pollute your life or purify your life. When you complain all the time, you are releasing poison into your life and you run positive people away. They tolerate you, but I'll let you in on a secret: They really do not want to be around you and try to avoid you. You're so busy being negative, you probably don't even realize it. Life's too short to be negative all the time.

Complaining is not based on your circumstances, it's based on the attitude of your heart. If you keep the right attitude during difficult times, if you keep your heart and mind open to positive possibilities instead of negative ones, good will eventually prevail. Don't let a complaining, negative outlook on life keep you from fulfilling your destiny and enjoying each day.

When you have a heart full of gratitude and maintain a positive outlook, it leaves little room to complain. You can always find something to be thankful for, no matter what the situation. If you believe it's going to be a bad day, trust me, it will be a bad day. You can speak it into existence. What you believe is what you'll receive. So from this day forward, look at the positive things and blessings you have right now in your life.

Choices

I challenge you each morning to consider two choices. You can choose to be in a good mood or a bad mood. I choose to be in a good mood. There was a period in my life when I used to let people upset me and ruin my day. I woke up one morning early on in life and realized I truly have choices.

One day, I called a dear true friend of mine—the late Lou Rosenfeld, who I called the Godfather—during one of those periods of anger. He was a big brother to me and owned a chain of record stores called Willies Records, named after his pet bird, Willie. I produced all of the radio and TV commercials for those stores from the chain's start in Richmond, giving them the slogan, "A hit's not a hit unless you get it from Willies." Sounds simple, but it created a chain of eleven record stores in three states. I was extremely upset and angry at someone or something one day, so I phoned Lou to vent about it. "Listen to yourself, Jay. You're giving up too much power." I said, "What do you mean, giving up too much power?" He said never give anyone or anything the power to upset your day like that. From that day forward, that's exactly what I did—I took back the power.

Make a choice to let it roll off of you and keep stepping. If someone knows they can upset you like that, you're giving them power to break you down. Each time something bad happens, you can choose to be a victim and let it ruin the rest of your day or you can choose to learn from it. I choose to learn from it.

Every time someone comes to you complaining, you can choose to accept their complaining or you can point out to them the positive side of life. Choose the positive side. You see, it's simple. Life is all about choices. Cut away all the junk that comes with it. You have the power to choose how you react to situations. You choose how people affect your mood. You choose to be in a good mood or bad mood. The bottom line: It's your choice how you live your life. Attitude, after all, is everything. Today is the tomorrow you worried about yesterday.

Tell The Truth

Stop lying. Stop lying to your friends. Stop lying to get what you want. Stop lying to bill collectors. Be honest. Stop lying to your husband or boyfriend. Stop lying to your girlfriend or wife. One lie leads to another. If you can't do something, just explain why. First of all, I tell the truth because the truth is easier to remember. You see, once you tell a lie you have to remember the details of that lie, then you have to tell another lie to cover that lie, setting yourself up to get caught. So why lie at all?

If you feel you have to be less than truthful about something, then just say nothing. Once you're known to tell lies, your reputation is shot among those who can do you some real good. No good person wants to be associated with a liar, so watch yourself and those you keep company with. They will lose trust in you. If you're telling lies, those who befriend you will most likely lie to you too.

You see, a lie gives you momentary satisfaction, but in the end, long-term pain and grief. The truth waits to be discovered, and it will be. Why put yourself in the embarrassing situation of having to face the truth because of your many lies. Tell the truth. It's never too late to start. You will earn respect, honor, love, admiration, and achieve success if you start by being truthful in all you do.

Stay Strong

Anyone can be positive, keep a good attitude, and stay happy and upbeat when things are going well, but what kind of attitude do you have when times get tough and things aren't going your way? Will you stay faithful and keep pressing on toward the goal even when it seems you're making no progress and those around you are discouraging you?

Sometimes trials and tough times enter your life to test you, make you stronger, and prepare you for the big blessing that's on its way. No matter how far you've been brought down, regardless of the severity of your troubles right now, if you keep the faith and stay strong you'll overcome them and come out a winner. You have to "go through to get to."

Anyone can quit. Anyone can complain. Anyone can make excuses. Anyone can get down and discouraged, but the real winner will persevere through the difficulties, through the storms, and past those who say you can't when you know you can. Stay strong. Be determined to prove yourself. Stay strong and fight the good fight. No can do it for you. You have to do it for yourself. So don't give up. Don't even think about.

Somebody's Watching You

Whether you realize it or not, people are watching you. If you have children, they're watching you. They watch how you dress. They watch how you take care of your home. They watch how you work. They watch how you take care of your health. They watch how you treat other people. They watch how you handle situations. People you're not aware of are watching.

Our children are watching us. If you're wondering why your kids are turning out the wrong way, maybe you should first look in the mirror. Although it's not always the case, you and the examples you set for them, the morals you fail to instill in them, may be the reason. What do you expose them to? Is it good for them and their future or are you just being selfish and don't care what they think, hear, or see. Do you let them get away with anything instead of putting your foot down when you need to? Children aren't supposed to raise themselves. That's not how it works. You're a parent, so do your job. Be responsible. Don't do it, and they'll cause you grief every time. Raise them well, and they'll make you proud.

Your children are watching you, your friends are watching you, and your supervisors at work are watching you. It's never too late to change for the better in whatever you do. Tomorrow's a new day. Make a new start. Let tomorrow be a new beginning. Start watching yourself.

Stop Procrastinating

If you're tired of falling behind and always playing catch-up, then make it a priority to get out in front of your life. It takes as much effort, sometimes more, to procrastinate than to get things done on time. Being punctual actually saves you from the anxiety that results from waiting until the last minute. There are the things you don't have to do today that you could still go ahead and get done. The further ahead you get, the more time you'll have to do what you enjoy. What needs to be done will not go away until completed. It lingers and causes stress. So why not do it now?

Instead of waiting for the week, day, or hour before the deadline to get started, go ahead, do it now, and get it behind you. Instead of dreading that approaching deadline and the task before you, choose to get it out of the way so you can stop thinking about it. Enjoy yourself and feel good knowing it's already been dealt with.

Once you begin to get a little bit ahead of where you need to be, the feeling is so positive, you'll be anxious to get even further ahead. Once you experience that feeling of not being rushed, you'll want to repeat that experience again and again. Then it becomes a welcomed habit.

Choose to live life on your own terms instead of always being weighed down by a deadline. No matter how old you are or how long you've put off a task, it's never too late to make a change for the better. Choose now to start getting done what needs to be done.

Take Better Care Of Yourself

We're all guilty of abusing our bodies. Sometimes it's on purpose, other times it's unknowingly. The bottom line is, if you treat your body with respect, you'll live a longer, healthier life. Even the Scriptures talk about staying fit, sleeping well, and eating the right foods. If you know you don't get enough sleep at night, go to bed earlier. You'll feel rested the next day. Get in that six-to-eight hours of sleep so your body can regenerate.

If you're on medications and have to alter your diet or follow specific instructions, then do the right thing. Practice some discipline so you can heal, rather than hinder the process. Take time out to pamper yourself. Get a massage, workout, or go to a spa every now and then. Moisturize your skin, drink at least half a gallon of water a day to keep your system hydrated. Start eating smaller, healthier portions of food to regulate your weight. Get regular medical and dental check-ups. Disease is dis-ease of the body.

Set aside time to relax and get away from it all just as you set aside time for the kids and business. When you make changes for your health's sake, you'll live longer, live healthier, and experience the abundant life that's waiting for you to arrive.

This Too Shall Pass

Life is filled with the unexpected. Just when things are going right, something unexpected happens. What started off as a wonderful day can instantly revert into a dark moment: If you just received the money you've been waiting for, the money that you were expecting to give you some breathing room, then a bill pops up that takes that cash away, know that more money will come, that the setback is temporary.

You've been in this situation many times, and you'll go through it again. You survived before and you'll survive again. Draw on the same strengths that got you through that last financial dilemma. Learn from that unexpected circumstance, and use what you've learned to prevent the next unexpected drain of funds from throwing you into a panic. Save more for a rainy day and spend less.

When things are going well, set up a financial cushion for yourself. Prepare for unexpected expenses. Always have something set aside for an emergency, because as you live, emergencies and unexpected situations that require your resources will arise when you least expect them. You'll be surprised by how much you can accumulate if you separate your wants from your needs. Learn from what's happening to you now. Define your financial priorities, prepare for next time, and don't stress about what's happening in your life right now because brighter days are ahead.

Don't Be So Defensive

Are you the kind of person who hates criticism? When matters of importance come up that need to be discussed, do you always think it's an attack? Life is not predictable. In business, friendships, and relationships, things you'd rather not deal with occur and must be dealt with to get past them. That's just life. So when the next conversation you don't want to have comes up, have a more open mind.

You have to be able to be talked to and to talk openly. When you become defensive when someone speaks to you, when you always think the conversation is an attack on you, you not only leave the issue open and unresolved, you discourage others from ever wanting to talk with you.

Listen before you jump for your gun and shoot someone down. Hear the other person out. Engage in a conversation, not an argument. You might learn something. You'll also find yourself becoming privy to more than has been shared with you before, because you're now more open-minded, less confrontational, and more approachable. Put the sword down. It's not always all about you when difficult or unpleasant things have to be discussed. Conversations about things you don't like shouldn't be a night at the fights.

Take Time Out For Yourself

Are you the person who's known to be good at taking care of your family, your friends, your work? Do you make sure everyone else is happy? That's fine and says a great deal about you as a person, but in doing that, are you neglecting to take care of yourself? Are you living like that today? You're helping everyone around you smell the roses, but you find yourself seldom catching the scent?

Do you spend all your time on other people, but not any on yourself? If you keep this up, as noble as it is, eventually you'll burn out and you won't be able to reach out to others. Decide today to begin investing in yourself. Set aside some time each day to do something nice, relaxing, rewarding, and enriching for you. If you style your own hair, go to the beauty salon or barber for a change. Get a manicure, pedicure, or spa treatment. Fly away for the weekend or treat yourself to that new outfit you've had your eye on.

Take time to relax and rejuvenate your body. When you're refreshed emotionally, physically, and spiritually, you are able to give to others more effectively. As you bring balance to your life, you will begin to enjoy it to the fullest and you'll discover the true champion within you. Be very careful not to burn yourself out and become drained by others because of your free heart. You deserve a break.

Watch Who You Walk With

Ever wonder why some people change from being good to being bad, nice to nasty, from being negative to becoming a more positive person? Well, there are many different reasons for that transformation. Some of it's life changes, some of it's spiritual changes. A lot of it's who you surround yourself with. If you're around very nice people, then the nice things begin to come out in you. If you place yourself in the company of nasty people, you pick up nasty traits. We adjust to our environment.

If you're trying to move forward in a positive way, then cut back on the time spent with negative friends and associates. A negative person will bring a positive person down much faster than a positive person can bring a negative person up. You can still love them, but until you get to a point of strength in your positive new life to handle negativity with a degree of strength, love your negative friends from a distance. Ever heard the saying misery loves company? Well, it's true. It does. Negative people want someone to agree with them and see things their way—dark, with no hope for change. They are always frustrated, angry at the world, themselves, and those who they feel are holding them back. In reality, they are holding themselves back. If you really want to stay on a positive path toward a bright future filled with wonderful possibilities and blessings, surround yourself with people who have a positive outlook on life.

Don't Be So Mean

When things don't go your way, do you throw a fit? When a date is set, do you agree to one thing then apply pressure before the deadline? Look back over your dealings in the past. If things turned out as planned, most likely they will again. If you've been dealing with the same person for a long period of time, you know they'll come through. Stop pushing the envelope. Wait. Life is uncertain, and things sometimes come up that delay the end result. You know this, so why do you start bugging that person early? Wait. Be patient.

When you want to know what's going on in a touchy situation, do you fly off the handle before you hear the complete explanation? Stop being so quick to anger. It's a turnoff and causes good people to avoid dealing with you because you're so quick tempered. How many times have you gone off and said something you regretted later because you didn't wait for the full explanation? Calm down. Wait. Listen to the full answer before you make an improper judgment and snap back. Stop blaming your temper on stress. Stop blaming it on the scars of the past. Stop using it to control someone because you're so insecure. It's time for you to move pass all of that and start living a peaceful life. Stay mean and soon you'll be lonely. Stop hassling, barking, and verbally abusing others around you when things don't go your way. The world does not revolve around you. Life is too short. If you can't control your temper, then get some help.

Is It Worth It?

Ever find yourself in a situation where your first thought told you not to do something? In places where you feel uncomfortable just because you want to fit in with the crowd? In the company of people with bad intentions you never planned on being around because you were with someone else? If you're compromising your beliefs, your better judgment, your nature, and doing things you said you'd never do, and you know it's wrong, the consequences of your actions and decisions could be damaging, painful, and irreversible.

Is it worth hurting someone you love? Is it worth jeopardizing your health? Is it worth exposing yourself to a lifestyle you know is morally wrong? Is it worth the thrill? Is it worth risking your life? Is it worth the high? Is it worth risking your reputation? Is it worth embarrassing your family? Is it worth losing your job? Is it worth compromising your values? Is it worth the pain and anger?

You'd better think about what you're doing right away and why you're doing it. If you know you don't like it, it could lead you into trouble. If it makes you uncomfortable, then stop before it's too late. Turn away from it while you can. Don't do this to yourself. Life has way too many joys to offer. If it's hard being there in your quest to break free, then stay away from the who, what, when, and where that keeps you in that vicious cycle of confusion and destruction.

Keep Your Word

As the saying goes, your word is your bond. In life it's more than true and can determine success, failure, peace, confusion, happiness, or sadness. Your reputation rests on your word. Some of us are too quick to say yes without thinking, only to later have to take it back and explain why you said "yes" in the first place. Is that you? Do you say just anything to get what you want for the moment, only to do the opposite when it's all said and done? Stop destroying your reputation.

When you say you're going to do something, make sure you can deliver before committing, then follow through. There are some things in life you only have one of. Among the most important of those is your reputation. A good reputation will take you a long way. If you lie about things, your business and personal life may never recover. If your word is good, you'll prosper in business, in relationships, and personal life.

It's understood that sometimes things happen that prevent you from following through on your promises. If that happens, inform the person to whom you made the promise as soon as possible. Give them a chance to make other arrangements. Don't wait until the last minute to let your inability to keep a promise be known. Make life easier. If you truly want to be happy and successful in life, say what you mean and mean what you say. If not, then don't say it at all.

Clean House

At the end of each year, take time to get rid of things and people that mean you no good, the things taking up space in your life. If you've got someone's number in your cell phone and you haven't received a call from them all year, delete it. If they were a true friend they would have called you at least once. Unless it's business, you don't have to throw the number away. Put it in your personal phone book. Don't continue to carry around the number of someone who never remembers your birthday or calls only when they want something.

Are old things cluttering up your room, office, closets, and basement? Sort out the junk and get rid of the excess. Still got an eight-track or cassette player in the room that you never use? You can't buy the tapes anymore anyway. Still holding on to that size three dress when you know you're a nine now? Unless you're on a serious workout program to get back down to a three, let it go. Remove the clutter.

Are there backstabbing or freeloading people in your life? You can't truly call them friends, so why be aggravated? Let them go! Are nosey people whose personal lives are a mess all into your business? Cut them off. Why be bothered? All of this is holding you back. They're distractions from an enemy that keeps you from the glorious promise that has been set aside for you.

Work On The Little Things

If you really wish to develop into a better person each day, I have a few simple things to share with you. For instance, instead of putting off reading the mail, read it now, keeping what you need, then dispose of the rest. Break this habit, and that pile of papers over on your desk, on the floor, or in the corner will no longer exist. Clean as you go when cooking, and you won't have a mess later. Then you can really enjoy the meal and relax afterward.

If something small needs to be done around the house or in your life, get it done. Release the pressure. Get it out of the way. If you work in the small things in your life, you'll have the room and strength to deal with the unexpected things coming your way. And they are coming. Manage what you can.

Has the gentleman in you run away from home? Start opening the doors and pulling out the chair for your lady and the beautiful woman who blew your mind may come back into your life. Kiss him as soon as he walks in the door instead of hitting him with a honey-do list. Listen to what's being said instead of waiting for the first opportunity to enforce your opinion. Be quiet and listen. Then after you've been heard, you listen. To better handle the big things in life, you first have to manage the small ones.

Think Before You Spread It

Ever pass on what you heard to someone else only to find your information was wrong because the person who told you had the wrong information? You meant no harm, but you caused it by passing on non-truths. You recklessly participated in damaging a person's character. The good perception someone once had has now been changed because they believed you. The damage you cause by passing on a rumor leaves a nasty residue. Each action has an influence that spreads far beyond its original context. Treat hearsay and gossip like fire. Don't spread it.

If you speak ill of others, beware! Karma is a mutha! If you backbite and backstab to damage someone's character, watch yourself. What you dish out will come back to you. It may not happen right away, but somewhere down the line, maybe years from now, something will happen in your life and you'll ask yourself, "Why me?" You may have become a changed person by then, but when it comes to karma, what goes around comes around.

When the talk starts, just walk away. Why sit and listen to rumors, slander, hearsay, and accusations? It doesn't enrich your life, nor do you any good, so what's the point? Would you like it if they were talking about you? Besides, what good does it do you anyway? To make matters worse, by participating in it, you become the very person the people you gossip to now distrust. Why? Because you did it to someone else, you can do it to them, and they know it.

How Long

Having trouble resting? Getting sick more than usual? Do you find yourself irritable, depressed, and angry more often? Have you been gaining or losing weight lately? If physical or medical problems aren't the cause, then maybe it's the lack of truth in you. When are you going to start being totally honest with yourself and the people in your life? If it doesn't set right with you, get it out. Stop holding it in. How long can you keep living like this? How long will you keep yourself miserable while making someone else happy? How long will you suppress your feelings and hold your tongue when you know you should say something? How long will you watch a bad situation grow when you know you can stop it by just being honest and open? Stop walking around in silence. Stop being so afraid to express your feelings. Maybe this is why you can't sleep at night and your resistance is low. Maybe this is the cause of your yelling for no reason, your short temper, and crying in the dark. You aren't being you anymore. You've forgotten who you are. How much longer can you do this before it destroys you?

If you're living someone else's life at the expense of your own and you can't take it anymore, don't be afraid to say what you really feel. Break the chains that bind you. Break the chains that are preventing you from being free. You've forgotten what it's like to be you. There's a thing called life that has been sitting on the front porch of your world waiting for you to come outside and enjoy it. Be honest with yourself, starting right now. How much longer will it take before you start living again?

Take A Look At Yourself

Whether your world is confused right now or going great, it's a good practice to periodically step back from yourself far enough to get a good look at how you're dealing with life. You often give good advice to others, but when you find yourself in the same situation it's sometimes hard to adjust and cope. If you step out of yourself and take a look, what will you see? Look at the way you spend your time. What would you change? How would you do things differently once you've taken the time to observe the real you? You know what's in your heart. How would you react to the way you treat people, the things you say to others, and the way you say it? If you were dealing with you in that regard, how would you like it? Would you like what you just said to someone else if it had been said to you? How would you feel if someone did to you what you just did to them? If you've never tried this exercise, try it sometimes. You'll be amazed at how you feel and what you see once you step out of the picture frame. Once you inventory yourself, you may find the keys to open doors of solution to your current group of concerns. It may provide the key to eliminating the issues you're facing and the drama you've endured. Taking a look at who you're becoming may provide you with a solution to get to the next level of your existence. None of us is perfect, and you need to remind yourself that that's okay as long as you continue to strive toward perfection with good intentions. We're all a work in progress.

Take Some Time Out For Yourself

Are you always doing for others, running errands, or bogged down with more work than you can handle? If you let these things overwhelm you, you'll eventually burn out or boil over from the stress. Your personality will sour, your health may suffer, and your personal relationships could become permanently damaged from all of the pressure. If those around you are telling you over and over to take a break and pay attention, do it before you cause yourself unnecessary problems.

You fit into this category if you work ten or more hours a day every day, if you have more to do than you can handle in your free time, if you do everyone's work including yours because you can't trust others to do it right. You're also in this category if you're having health problems related to stress, if you can't say something positive when people ask you how you're doing, if your temper has become shorter, or if your love life is suffering because of the workload. If any of this applies to you, break the cycle by taking a break.

Step away from it all. Take a vacation, not a visit to see friends or family—a real vacation. This will give you the opportunity to really look at life and realize it's not all about work and running around constantly. There's a beautiful world out here waiting for you to slow down and enjoy. What good is working so hard if you get sick from it or never taste the fruits of your labor? Don't put it off until later. Make plans now to take a break from the stress, recharge, and look closely at your life and the things in it that matter.

Don't Get So Mad About It

Do you throw things or yell when you're upset? Get nervous and short of breath? Do you stay mad for days or get violent? Why? If you throw something, you'll break it, creating another problem. Yelling doesn't help the situation. It only further upsets the person you're yelling at. If you verbally or physically abuse a person, they will avoid dealing with you or leave you. That includes keeping things from you and doing things behind your back to avoid your anger. If that's not what you want, then stop the madness. Things happen and will happen that you don't like in life, so accept them and deal with them calmly. Enough yelling. Kill the bad temper.

A rise in blood pressure out of anger can kill you. Staying angry for more than a few hours only keeps you miserable while the rest of the world enjoys life. Don't assume your anger has that much power over someone else. It really doesn't. Or at least it shouldn't unless the other person is fragile enough to let it. It has the most power over you because you let it control you instead of you controlling it. Get over it. Aren't you sick and tired of saying I'm sorry?

If you're the violent type, keep it up and you're on your way to jail. It's just a matter of time, if it hasn't happened already. A person can only take so much physical abuse before they turn on you, leave you, or take you out. Hitting someone because you're angry is wrong anyway you look at it. So, the next time you feel like you're losing control, take a walk, call someone, or get some professional help.

Decide To Have A Good Day

How each day turns out is ultimately up to you. What happens around you may be uncontrollable, but how you react to it is controllable. It's up to you. You can let the events of the day dictate how you feel about it or you can dictate how you feel about the day. Choose to feel good about each day because the very fact you're here to see it is in itself a blessing. When you awaken each morning, you're already a winner because you've been given another chance to try it again. Another chance to give it your all and be the best you can be. You're given a wonderful opportunity each day.

If something happens to your car, don't let that ruin your day. It's a machine. It needs attention and maintenance. If you're not in a position to handle what you have, then why have it? If you can't take care of it, then don't buy it until you can. If it means you have to go without it for a while, then so be it. Don't let your wants force you beyond the reality of your means. You'll get there in time. If a co-worker or supervisor irritates you, instead of fighting back, learn to let it roll off you, and go on doing what you were employed to do to the best of your ability. Decide to have a good day no matter what.

Never let someone else or something else turn your day into an emotional disaster. That's giving up too much power. This and every day is a gift, so refuse to let things saturate your thoughts to the point where you're not enjoying life.

Have Some Fun

When life gets too hectic, and it seems to crowd you into a corner, be very careful not to make yourself sick trying to do it all without taking a break to breathe. If you're not careful, you'll find yourself forsaking the other things around you that need your attention. Things like family, friends, your companion, children, and your home. Pleasure is one of the best remedies to combat feeling ill, depressed, and stressed. When life becomes too much for you, take a break.

Think about it. When was the last time you engaged yourself in your favorite pastime? You used to swim, bowl, bike, camp, go to the park, shoot pool, play cards, cook on the grill, play tennis, paint, work in the garden, play ball, go sailing, and relax on the beach from time to time, but now you're too busy to do those things. You're always saying year after year, "This summer I'm going to do this. This spring I'm going to do that," but you never get around to it because you fail to make the time. You'd be surprised at how much better you'll feel about life if you just take some time out for pleasure.

Do something you enjoy that has nothing to do with the situation or the circumstances that pressure you day to day. Find a hobby or rediscover a former passion, enjoy a shameless pleasure, go somewhere breathtaking and smile, laugh, love, and create wonderful memories you'll cherish for years to come. If you really want to feel like the work you do and the stress you endure each day is worth it all, enjoy yourself.

Enough Is Enough

Why are you killing yourself? If you're doing something detrimental to your health, I ask you and you should ask yourself, "Why? Why am I doing this to myself?" Ask yourself this over and over until you get tired and just stop. If you don't stop it, whether it's drugs, alcohol, or cigarettes, whatever it is, it will eventually stop you. It's been so long since you had a physically pure life, you don't remember what it feels like. You've become what you consume, and you're so use to it that the way you feel each day is now the new norm. In reality, it's slowly killing you physically and mentally. You don't need those things to be happy. Stop the madness.

It may be something you do socially. It may be something everyone else, but you, sees destroying you. Maybe it's something you do secretly behind closed doors. It's your dark secret. You've got it under control. Check yourself before you wreck yourself. If you can't do it alone, then get some help. It's out there everywhere. Save yourself. In order to get on the road to a better life, you have to make a change for the better by avoiding the bad.

Not only are you hurting yourself, you're hurting those around you with your destructive habit. They are silently crying for you. Whatever it is, stop letting this habit drain you, your finances, your health, and your life of its destiny. Who has the power, you or it? Quit the bad once and for all. The toughest step to take is the first one. It's not easy, but you can do it. You can have the happiness you see around you and all that comes with it if you just put your mind to it and take control.

Know When To Say No

How do you deal with saying yes when you really mean no? Do you agree to something when in reality you don't want to do it? Do you find yourself compromising how you really feel just to keep the peace or to get someone out of the way for the moment? The problem with that is you're not being true to yourself, and as a result, you find yourself feeling unhappy because you allowed something bad or unwelcome to happen. Sometimes you have no choice, but in most cases you do. Decide what's most important before you give your answer. Stop giving the green light to things you don't want to occur in your life. It's your life.

You know your partner spends too much money, so why say yes when you know you'll hit the ceiling when the bill comes. You know you're going to hate going out of your way once again for a friend who never repays the favor. You know hanging out tonight is not a good idea because you have a big meeting tomorrow that you need to be prepared for. Maybe you've been given the chance to take advantage of a great deal, but you know you're already under the financial eightball with more money going out than coming in. No matter how sweet the deal is, don't do it. There'll be another deal at another time. Taking this one will only make your financial situation worse.

Being true to yourself will give you peace and the respect of those around you. You'll sleep better and feel better. It may hurt or disappoint some people or make them uncomfortable when you don't agree to some things, but as they say, the truth will set you free. Stop saying yes if you really don't mean it.

Hang On Before You Hang Up

Have you ever talked to someone on the phone and, for whatever the reason, had to hang up before the conversation was completed? If you've been in this situation, you received some but not all of the point the person on the other end attempted to bring across. As a result, you find yourself only understanding whatever was discussed within what you've been told. The problem is this, the conversation wasn't finished. You didn't hear it all. You didn't get all the facts, so your conclusion may be wrong and uninformed. Listen the next time someone says, "I want to talk to you." Be quiet and truly listen. Let them get what they have to say out of their system before you try to chime in with your opinions. If you're wondering why someone won't open up to you anymore, maybe it's because you never let them finish saying what's on their mind before you start telling them what they're thinking. Listen when someone's trying to speak to you. Stop jumping to conclusions just because someone's pattern or actions have more than often been the same. No matter how much you think you know a person, there's always a possibility in the grand scheme of things that they've changed. If they haven't, you'll know it. Hear them out.

You may be asking to yourself, "Why listen?" If you didn't want to hear what they have to say, then why are you giving that person the opportunity to talk to you in the first place? You gave them an audience.

If It's Not What You Want, It Is What It Is

If you've asked for honesty and have received it, then accept it. If you can't accept the honesty, then don't ask for it. The truth comes with a big responsibility. After you get the truth you seek in a situation, then you have to respect it. You may not like it, but you have to respect it.

Sometimes you want things to be your way. You want a person or persons around you to feel the way you feel. That may happen, but it also may take some time. Waiting requires patience. You can become so impatient in the waiting process that you run what could have been what you wanted and needed away from you, then you feel rejected because you didn't get what you felt you deserved. Stop pushing others to do what you want and feel the way you feel. They're not you.

Sometimes we fall accidentally. Sometimes we fall on purpose. Sometimes we fall due to circumstances. No one ever promised your life would be fair. Sometimes it is and sometimes it isn't. In order for you to make it through this journey called life, you have to accept things for what they really are and not what you want them to be.

If You Know It's A Mess, Stay Out Of It

Too often, we tend to get involved in situations that just aren't healthy. I know you mean well, but sometimes you should not get involved. If someone is in need and you have the resources to help them, then do so. The blessing you are to them will come back to you many times over. But don't do it to get something in return. Don't feel like you have to help everyone. Some people are so toxic or destructive that helping them will hurt you.

If someone asks for help out of a self-imposed bad situation that has them in all kinds of trouble, ask yourself, "Do I want to be associated with this and bring this drama into my life? Will it bring me down? Will it harm my reputation?" You make your own decision. I'm only urging you to think about these things before you jump at the opportunity to get involved in a bad situation.

If it's a ticking time bomb, then why are you getting involved? They're calling you because the flames are heading their way. Even if you have a chance to profit from it, you could be walking into something you don't need to be involved in. Instead of beating yourself up after the fact for sticking your nose where it really didn't belong, don't get involved. Think with your head, not your heart. Give advice if you want to help, but don't jump into dirty water. You will not come out clean.

Turn It Off

We've become a society of "right now." Everything happens right away. Thirty years ago, if you called someone and they were on the phone, you'd get a busy signal and you'd have to wait until they got off the phone and put it back on the hook before you could talk to them. You had three or four local channels to watch. After they signed off after midnight, you went to sleep. If you wanted to know what happened overnight, you had to wait on the morning newspaper or newscast. Now you get information every second on your iPad, cell phone, PC, or on hundreds of cable channels. You can reach anyone, anywhere, anytime in the world by cell phone, e-mail, BlackBerry, and video conferencing. Today, if you miss something, it's because you want to. Sometimes you need to because it's overpowering you and you have no time for yourself. Turn off that cell phone if you're trying to get something done and it's distracting you.

You've got the Bluetooth glued to your ear, in the store, the bathroom, the gym, on vacation, the office, the car, while you spend time with your family and kids, fishing, jogging, on the golf course, in meetings. If you have the phone on while you sleep, ready to wake up just to take a call—if this is you, and you're running around with your head cut off, start giving the important things and people around you as well as yourself some uninterrupted quality time and respect. The world will be fine without you for a few hours. It survived thirty years ago. Taking time out for you and what's important in your life is necessary in order for you to maintain order in your life. Don't get me wrong. If you've got business to handle, handle it, but when the demand is too great and the cell phone is driving you crazy, when you know you need "me" time, turn the cell phone off.

Sometimes You Just Have To Understand

Have you called someone recently to ask for help only to be told no or not now? You may have gotten that answer for reasons other than the one you may be thinking of. If you've asked a favor of a friend who you've helped in the past, only to be denied, they really may not be able to help you. Don't assume they're being cold or selfish because they don't have time at that moment to talk, meet, help, or listen to you. They may have a good reason, one they can't share with you. The world doesn't stop just because you have a need. It keeps turning.

Don't make the mistake of taking "no" or "I can't" personally. If you're asking for money, maybe they can't loan it to you because they have financial obligations or challenges of their own. If you want to talk and you're told it's a bad time, maybe they're just exhausted and need to shut down to recharge for another day of life. It may have been a hard day or maybe they're busy enjoying something else at the moment.

Don't be rude. First, ask the person you're speaking to if they're busy right now. Is this a good time to talk? They really may want to help you but just can't take anything else on right now. You've been in that situation before. So don't feel like because you are having an emergency, the person you're talking to has to make it their emergency. They don't have to and may not want to. It doesn't mean they're being selfish or dislike you. Sometimes the timing isn't right for them to get involved or give you assistance.

It's Up To You

If you think waiting on someone else to change will solve your problems, you can forget that theory. Your happiness or success does not and should not depend on the actions of someone else. The way to get past your problems is to make changes for the better within yourself. Advice is good sometimes, but if taking someone's advice has gotten you where you are, and it's not a nice place, then stop listening. Stop relying so much on what others say you should do. It's up to you.

The problem is not the situation you're in. The problem is the way you're dealing with it. If the way you handle things gets you the same unwanted results, then change the way you interpret the situation and handle it differently. The problem is not the way you are treated by someone else. The problem is how you allow the way they treat you to affect you. What happened in the past is not the problem. It's the fact that you're letting that past hold you back by allowing what happened yesterday or years ago to affect you today. It's over. You can't go back and change it. Treating it like it happened today is keeping you attached to the problem.

Take responsibility for your problems, then you'll regain control of them and be well on your way to solving them. In every aspect of life, it's up to you to get what you want, accomplish what you've set out to achieve, and go where you want to go. You have every resource available to you to get there if you just open your eyes and listen to your heart, whether you get there or past this point in life.

Say Nothing At All

Backbiting and saying untruthful things about others is wrong. As my mother always said to me, "If you can't say something good about a person, say nothing." If you can't wait to get to the phone to spread the latest gossip, if you slander those you dislike just to hurt them, what you do will come back to you. Just because someone said something untrue or distasteful about you doesn't mean it's right to do the same. Sometimes you have to respond for damage control, but most of the time it's best to ignore the comment and let it fade away. Not retaliating is hard to do when someone won't stop talking badly about you. But in time, if you refuse to add logs to the fire of accusations, negative comments and lies, that fire will go out. Ignore what's been said if you know there's no truth in it. You have nothing to defend if it's a lie. Getting to the point where this stuff doesn't affect you takes time, but you'll get there with practice. Those around you who believe lies about you aren't your true friends anyway. If the accusations don't match up with your actions, it'll be forgotten. Responding to gossip and lies just keeps them alive. Don't dignify them with a response. Say nothing at all.

If You Want It Give It

Are you a taker? You may be one and not realize it or maybe you don't want to. If you've always been catered to in life, if you're used to having the best and expecting the best, that's okay if you're willing to give freely of yourself and resources in return for the kindness and consideration being bestowed upon you. I like the best and having nice things given to me and done for me like anyone else. But problems develop over time when you fail to do the same in return.

I'm not referring to merely monetary or physical things. I'm also talking about your time and feelings. If you always want someone to do what you want, but you're seldom willing to do what they want, check yourself. If you want to be listened to you when you have something to say, but you refuse to hear it when there's something on someone else's mind, check yourself. If you desire affection and attention, then you must be willing to give it as well without conditions. You can't expect to keep taking from others and never giving of yourself.

If you feel you're losing someone dear to you, if you feel like love is slowly packing up and leaving you, maybe it's because you're taking too long to give back. It hurts to leave someone you love when the answer to the problem is so simple, but you've got to do what you've got to do when the other person just doesn't get it. If you find some of what I've said applies to you, change your ways before it's too late to save what little you have left. Start Feeling Good About Yourself.

You are beautiful. Whether you believe it or not, you truly are. You're unique. You're one of a kind. No one can do what you do like you do. No one can love like you do. No one thinks like you do. There is only one you. Never put yourself down or let someone else cause you to think less of yourself. Anyone who does this does not love you unconditionally, even if they say they do. If you love someone, never try to break them down no matter what the situation. You are truly a gift to this world so Start Feeling Good About Yourself.

Right now there's someone in your life depending on you to be there for them. They need you. You look good so take care of yourself each day. When you're dressed and enter a room, all eyes are on you because you look good in what you wear. You do your job better than anyone else, so always give it your best shot and strive to do it even better tomorrow. Even when things get a little off course, you're still on top of it because you make it through. You have so much to give so give it every chance you get because you're loved when you feel good about yourself.

There's someone who looks forward to seeing you each day. They're happy just to be around you. You have it within yourself to do and be whatever you want in this life, so from this moment forth, just put your mind to it and do it. Don't let anyone anywhere tell you what you can or cannot achieve. Continue to grow closer to your destiny, and you'll realize all of your dreams.

Epilogue

The Best Is Yet To Come

We all have the ability to be great built within us. Sometimes, you just sometimes need a little help getting it to the surface to grow and flourish. It is my hope that you'll keep this book around, refer to it from time to time as life happens, taking what you've learned throughout these pages and applying these lessons, motivational words, and reflections to your everyday life. Some things you have gone through, some you're going through now, and some are yet to come. Know that I love you and God loves you.

Let me leave you with this, the closing to my worldwide radio show each night on 88.1 WHOV and I-Heart Radio:

"Be kind to your friends, because you never know when you will need that friend again. Keep your head to the sky and your mind in a heavenly place. Remember you can be what you want to be and achieve whatever you want to achieve in life. Just put your mind to it and do it! And don't let the negative forces stop you because they will try. Just remember that love is the answer. Understanding is and always will be the key to success and someone greater than you and I is the ultimate solution to all of your problems. On that note, here's Red Roses on Your Pillow and Smooth Jazz All Over Your Radio."

Now. Go Take On The Day!

Contact The Author

Visit my website at www.wisdomfromthejazzman.com to get more life-enriching words of wisdom and to hear new, frequently updated motivational and inspirational audio clips to help you on your quest toward your destiny. You can also follow me on Twitter @jaylang1.

Acknowledgements

First, I have to give honor to my Lord and Savior, Jesus Christ, for giving me a new life and allowing me to be the vessel for this work of inspiration

To my family, all of you have been very supportive throughout my life, and for that, I thank you. You accept me for me, love me unconditionally, and have nurtured me along the way. To my Dad, my coach and confidant, you're always there for me no matter what the hour, just to talk when I need someone to hear me and listen. My love for you is enormous. You're my best friend above all others. To my sisters Deanna and Piccola, my big brother Jimmy, brother Eric, aunts, uncles, and cousins—thanks for the unconditional love. To my daughter, Kiara, you are my motivation, the reason I conquer life's obstacles, and you are the love of my life. Elisa, thank you for giving me a wonderful daughter and being a good mother. We did good! Aunt Frances, I've always admired your quiet courage and peace. I love you. Keep my room ready. Uncle Ronald and Uncle Hardy, the two of you are just too smooth and have taught me so much through your quiet strength. Aunt Beverly, keep making that monster corn pudding. And to all the strong women and friends who have passed through and contributed to my life, I wish I had enough room to mention you all. Thank you for all you've given me through your heart.

To my publisher, I thought of self-publishing but I wanted something greater than that for this work, and I needed an established publishing team working with me to do it. John Koehler at Koehler Books, thanks for giving me a shot, inviting me to your home, and assisting me in completing the task I have been charged with in getting this work out to the world. Thank you, David Hancock, founder of Morgan James Publishing. You are a truly good man with a vision we both see eye to eye on. Thanks for lunch. It was a meeting that set the wheels in motion. In the two of you I know I have two great new friends. God does not make mistakes. I'm looking forward to many more works to come with you and your hard-working publishing teams.

Special thanks to the people who have inspired me greatly in this life: Joyce Meyer, Joel Osteen, TD Jakes, my Pastor, John K. Jenkins Sr. of the First Baptist Church of Glenarden, Bishop Darryl Scott, Hampton University President Dr. William R. Harvey, my Facebook family of friends, Smokey Robinson, the late Isaac Hayes, Quincy Jones, the late Ray Charles, the late James "Uncle James" Brown, my spiritual big brother Tom Pope , Gwen Pope, Bill Washington, Dee Dee Hoover, Lonnie Liston Smith, Jim Watkins, Russell Simmons, the late Frankie Crocker, Boo "Daddy Boo"Frazier, Donnie Simpson, Steve Crumbley, Ben Tucker, Magic Johnson, the late Nat King Cole, the late John H. Johnson, Hassan the drummer, Kirk Franklin, David Grigsby, Jack Wellmon, Vernon Johnson, Charles Geer, Ernie Singleton, John Gray PhD, Nelson Mandela, the late Rev. Dr. Martin Luther King, Ghandi, Creflo Dollar, Kenneth Copeland, the late Barry White, Dennis Kimbro, Napoleon Hill, Og Mandino, Dr. Laura Schlessinger, and Ralph Marston.

To My Best Friends And Supporters:

Roger Parham, Leonard Walker, Khari Branch, Preston Mc-Ghee, Bob Baldwin, Ken Navarro, Allen Kempler, The Pastors Study (Kevin, John and Ray), Priscilla Holmes, Tony Winger, Linn R. Williams, Gina Darby (thanks for being there that day), Will Downing, Kelly Turner, Norman Brown, The Honorable Superior Court Judge JR Rigsby, Kenny King, Bernadine Simmons, my 96.3 WHUR family, Chris Cunningham, Phyllis Baker, Bill and Brad Eure, Rose Day and The Boys, James and Gloria Boone, Michael Steele, Barbara Ross (you were the first), Dana S.Hubbard, Ed Graves, Nathan Watts, James M. Robinson, Darin Swann, Becky Taylor, James and RaJean Taylor (we have many more sailing trips to go), Anthony Cogswell, Kenny King, Emanuel Payton, Diana Wilson, Dr. Lloyd M. Bonner, Camille Watson-Peay, Dr. Lawrence Hyman, Edward Jackson, Beth Jackson Hodges, Jonathan Carter (lil bro), Doris James, Carl Anderson, Blanche and James Champion, Janice Mitchell, Bill Morgan, Cynthia Norris, Lawrence and Pamela Robinson. There are so many more. I'm sure I've left someone out on this list, but you know who you are. Just blame it on my head, not my heart. Besides, I'll catch you on Vol.2.

CPSIA information can be obtained at www.ICGtesting.com
Printed in the USA
BVOW00s1109221013

334245BV00002B/24/P

9 781938 467240